ADULTING
— FOR BEGINNERS —

LIFE SKILLS FOR TEENS & YOUNG ADULTS WHO HAVE MOVED OUT

Want To Live Independently, Manage Their Money, Build Successful Careers & Ultimately Become A Grown-up

N. M. HILL

Copyright © 2023 N.M. Hill.

All rights reserved. This book is protected by copyright. No part of this book may be reproduced or transmitted in any form or by any means, including as photocopies or scanned-in or othwer electronic copies, or utilized by any information storage and retrieval system without written permission from the copyright owner.

Interior Design by Formatted Books

Printed in the United States of America.
ISBN: 978-1-7392414-2-1

DEDICATION

To all the teens and young adults out there, remember this:

Growing up is not about losing your imagination or sense of adventure. It's about finding new ways to dream, new paths to explore, and new heights to reach. So embrace the opportunities and challenges of adulthood with curiosity, courage, and grace. And never forget that the journey of self-discovery and fulfillment is a lifelong one, filled with endless possibilities and endless potential

Make yourself proud.

You are the future!

INNER CIRCLE

Would you like to be a part of my inner circle?

I have nothing to giveaway if you decide to sign-up.

There is no free ebook or worksheet which most likely you don't want anyway.

What I can promise is that by being a part of my inner circle you will receive random emails from me from time to time.

Some will be personal development related, some will be personal and some will just try and make you laugh or at the very least put a smile on your face!

I promise not to bombard you daily with emails to clog up your inbox. As a reader of my book and fellow human, I value and care about you too much.

You can unsubscribe at any time you've had enough.

Now, I'm guessing you know what to do with the below QR Code.

CONTENTS

Introduction ix

Chapter 01 1
The Flavor Formula: Unlocking Your Kitchen Potential

Chapter 02 21
*Surviving Emergencies: Essential Skills For
The Home, Road & Street Safety*

Chapter 03 43
DIY Movement: Home & Car Repair/Maintenance Skills

Chapter 04 59
*Priority Numero Uno: Taking Care Of
Your Mental & Physical Health*

Chapter 05 81
The Money Game: Achieve Financial Independence

Chapter 06 95
*Positive Connections: Developing
Interpersonal Skills For Everyday Life*

Chapter 07........................115
Dreams To Reality: Purposeful Goal Setting

Chapter 08........................131
The Career Blueprint: Crafting Your Path To Success

Conclusion........................149

9 Easy Recipes You Can Do Yourself........155

References........................165

INTRODUCTION

"When you're young, everything feels like the end of the world, but it's not; it's just the beginning."
—**ZAC EFRON**

You probably look at people older than you and feel equally impressed and shocked. There will always be people you aspire to and others you want to avoid. The great thing is you don't have to be like everyone else. You are responsible for creating your future life as you move through adulthood.

The critical thing to know is you can do anything in your life.

You only need to use your common sense and learn some crucial life skills to help you achieve your personal goals. You might already have achieved some important life goals but are looking to fill in some gaps. This situation is typical for everybody, as we all learn something new daily.

Look upon this book as the ultimate reference manual for your adult journey. You can skip things you know and go to the chapters where you need help. After all, why waste time on things you already know? It's about learning the skills you need to thrive and get the best out of your life.

Where Are You Right Now?

You might be surprised at the answer if you ask yourself this question. Your life consists of many different areas, but they are all connected. It's all about finding the right balance in your life. Then you can ensure that you grow in all the essential areas of your life.

- You might want to further your career and don't know where to start.
- Relationships are confusing, and you can't connect with different people.
- You tried to set up a home and had to move back to your parents' house.
- You sometimes feel physically and emotionally stressed with daily activities.

The list goes on and continues to grow as you get older. It's all about understanding what you can and can't do. You might have tried already and failed to achieve your goals. But don't let that stop you from starting again. You can start your new journey by flipping it around and viewing it as a life adventure.

There are no boundaries to what you can do in your life. Only the ones that you make for yourself. This book is your handy companion to help you along the way. You can take the information you are missing and use it to move forward. You will show everybody you have the abilities and the mentality to make a happy life.

Dealing With Daily Challenges And Struggles In A Better Way

In your late teens and twenties, you are still figuring out who you are and what you want to do. It's perfectly natural to feel this way. I grew up in a pretty large family with six siblings. Their children (my nieces and nephews) have all worked through college and university and got jobs. I also have three children of my own so I can completely empathize with the obstacles that are thrown at you - here are a few:

- ★ You feel stressed when studying and in your early career, which sometimes affects your mental and physical health.
- ★ You are frustrated with having little or no money, which stops you from buying things you want or having life experiences.
- ★ You have to deal with societal pressure to achieve things by a certain age, such as buying a house, having a career, etc.
- ★ You want to excel in your life but don't know how to set and achieve goals to realize your ambitions.
- ★ You need the proper knowledge to do things by yourself and worry if you will fail.

These feelings are real and can hurt you to your core. You want to do things but can feel restricted by your parents and other adults. You appreciate their help, but you want to start doing things yourself. It can be hard to explain how you feel, which makes it worse. You need your own space so you can grow and spread your wings.

We learn from our mistakes, and that's what helps us grow.

It's impossible to get it right every single time. But if you reduce your mistakes, you will have more success in life. Why give yourself extra work and problems? You can proactively use the life skills I have detailed in each chapter to help you. Don't forget, if you know something already, move on to what you don't know in the book.

Moving Into Adulthood Is Special

You are about to create a life that has been waiting for you. Imagine sitting in your home, with money in the bank, working through your dream career. You can also enjoy positive relationships with all your family members and friends. It is possible to have it all if you are prepared to learn and grow.

Adulthood doesn't suck. It's all about doing it right.

I will empower you to help you thrive in life. You will learn essential life skills to help you achieve happiness and success. You can gain the confidence to deal with anything thrown at you, whatever happens in your life. Get ready to start setting and achieving positive goals, and embrace your adulthood now.

01

THE FLAVOR FORMULA: UNLOCKING YOUR KITCHEN POTENTIAL

> *"A recipe has no soul, you as the cook must bring soul to the recipe."*
> **—THOMAS KELLER**

The power of food and cooking is an untapped resource for many. Learning to cook can open up your world like never before. It's a great way to connect with people in your life. Think back to a time when you were ill. What did your Mom or Dad do? Your parents probably made your favorite dish - the food connection.

Food can help you nurture relationships.

It's the perfect way to express love. Have you ever made a meal for someone you love? Learning to cook could ramp up your relationship-building skills. When you take the time and effort to cook for someone, it's always remembered. A partner, family member, or friend will usually remember a meal you cooked due to the effort and personal touch required.

Go down in history and create your first signature dish.

You can also learn how to make your favorite food. There are plenty of recipes online that you can access easily. Most of them detail the difficulty level, so you can start on easy ones and work your way up. What you thought was your favorite food might become something completely different.

It's also a great way to save money. Moving out and creating a home on your own costs money. Anything you can do to keep it is worth it. Eating out at restaurants and buying fast food can all add up, especially with the current cost of living. Eating out twice a day, seven days a week, could cost you $448 to $672 a month if not more.

Not only will you save vast amounts of money, but there are many other benefits:

- You can save valuable time. You don't have to wait for the delivery guy or wait for your meals in a restaurant.
- You can prepare things in advance and grab them when you want them.
- You also have more control over what goes inside your meal, so you can ensure you are eating as healthy as possible.
- You can put the wow factor into your food with home cooking.

It can be soul-destroying eating the same bland, frozen meals. Remember how unhealthy most of these pre-prepared meals can be. Homemade cooking trumps frozen food every time. It has its own feel and distinct taste. You can also make extra and freeze some for another day. At least your frozen food will be top-notch!

Once you have made a few easy recipes, you can start getting more serious. Try out some more challenging recipes and taste the difference. You'll begin to appreciate food more and will understand what herbs and spices go with what food. You can then take it to the next level and create your own meals.

Showcase your new skills with a dinner party.

You'll also be able to use your new cooking skills wherever you are. You won't have to feel embarrassed about cooking ever again. You can host your first dinner party with your newfound confidence in cooking. Invite your family or friends around and cook your signature dish. Nothing tastes better than eating food cooked by somebody else.

Cooking is only one of the things you need to learn, as it also comes with other skills. You need to know what to buy when heading to the grocery store. Then once you have the food, you need to know how to store it correctly. Meat, vegetables, and fruit must be dealt with differently to ensure they are fresh and ready to use.

Are you already buying food and know your way around? If so, then move on to the next chapter. This chapter will help you buy groceries and store them properly. I'll remove the confusion from expiration dates, so you get the most from your food.

I've also added a few simple, easy recipes at the end of the book to get you started!

Grocery Shopping Made Simple

You've arrived at the grocery store and don't know what to buy. There are so many choices you don't know where to start. You can already feel the stress getting to you. Luckily, you don't need to think like this. Before you go to the store, write a shopping list for what you need. Once you've made a list, stick to it like glue.

Create The Best Shopping List

You can follow these points to ensure your shopping list covers everything. It will make your first shopping trip as easy as possible for you:

- ★ List any items you know you 100% need right now
- ★ Add the brand of the item if you have a preference for a particular one
- ★ Make a note of the quantity you need so you don't over or under-buy an item
- ★ Save lots of time by grouping similar items together, e.g., canned goods
- ★ Put fresh things together and grab these at the end of your shop

If you're making a particular recipe, you need everything to make it correctly. A shopping list helps you stay organized and ensures you don't forget anything. Nobody wants to make another trip back to the grocery store. The grouped items on the list also help you to save time by going to the same aisle or section.

Using a shopping list is also crucial to budgeting. Many supermarkets deliberately place items in strategic places to make people buy more. A list helps you stay within your shopping budget, as you won't overspend. It will make your shopping experience better than ever before. You are saving money, time, stress, and energy.

Head To The Bread And Egg Sections First

Another tip is to go straight to the bread and egg sections of the grocery store. These items are the most popular as they are essentials. Consequently, they are the items that grocery stores tend to run out of first. Remember to store them well in your basket or cart to stop your bread from getting squished or breaking any eggs.

Canned Goods And Packaged Food

The next food to go to in the store would be non-perishables (canned goods) and packaged food. These items will not get squished like your bread or leak like fresh food. Also, they are usually the heaviest items you will buy. Therefore, you can put them at the bottom of your cart.

Remember when you listed things by the aisle on your list? Now is the time you can take advantage of that as well. You can start shopping by aisle. It will help to speed up your shopping trip. You are already ¾ of the way through your shopping list. **You'll be heading out the exit before you know it!**

Examine Fresh Food With An Imaginary Microscope

Fresh food might taste yummy, but it is also a potential health hazard if you don't check it for freshness. According to the World Health Organization (WHO), an estimated 600 million (almost 1 in 10 people globally) fall ill after food poisoning, and 420,000 die yearly.

Examining your fresh food is critical. Using your senses is a sure way to check if something is fresh. It might not be the most pleasant thing to use your nose. But it will let you know if something is rotten. It's always better to be safe than sorry. Here are some more pointers you can use as well:

Beef

Fresh meat, such as beef, should not feel slimy when you touch it. You should also check that the meat has no unpleasant smells. The color of beef should always be red. If not, give it a miss!

Fish

Don't get squeamish, but you'll need to look at the eyes. The fish's eyes should be clear and bulging, not cloudy or red. The scales need to be tight to the skin, and there should be no slime. If you press the body with your thumb, it should spring back.

Other Kinds Of Seafood

If you want to shop for other types of seafood, you need to rely on your senses. Ideally, shellfish should be bought alive. The shells of prawns and shrimps should be firm, and the heads attached firmly. Also, check that there are no unpleasant odors.

Chicken

Chicken is a different kettle of fish! You need to look at the chicken breasts and check if they are firm to the touch. Check that the chicken skin is attached to the meat. Finally, ensure it does not smell chemical, have a strong odor, or feel slimy.

Spots Are Never Good

Fruits and vegetables are sensitive, so when examining them, ensure you don't press hard on them or pinch them. Otherwise, the same areas will develop bruises or black spots. Using your eyes and nose to check them for freshness is better. Not to mention, people might have already been pressing and pinching them.

Avoid fruits (including tomatoes) with black, sunken spots or soft spots. Also, don't buy any leafy vegetables when the leaves are yellow, wilting, or have brown spots. The leaves should be crisp and bright - lettuces and cabbages are best with tight leaves. Root crops, like potatoes and carrots, should always be hard.

Be Careful With Raw Chicken

You might already be aware of the potential hazards of raw chicken. However, it is always worth mentioning again. When you arrive at the cash register, always separate your fresh food from raw chicken. For food safety reasons, keep it separate from your other purchases, especially ready-to-eat food.

How To Store Your Food The Right Way

Now you have your food. You need to get the most from it. Storing it well will help you do this and make the food taste as fresh as possible.

Storing Vegetables

Here are some ways in which you can store different vegetables. Also, important information about how long you can keep them and how you can freeze them.

Leafy Greens

Examples of leafy greens are kale, spinach, lettuce, bok choy, and swiss chard. Leafy greens last longer if you rinse them and then wrap them in a paper towel or tea towel. Then you can put them in a container or a sealed plastic bag in the refrigerator.

Asparagus

Always store asparagus in the fridge. You can wrap the stalks in a damp paper towel to keep them moist. Alternatively, you can put the stalks upright and store them in a cold glass of water.

Root Vegetables and Squash

Store root vegetables and squash outside the fridge or in a cool, dark, and dry spot. A cupboard is a perfect place to store them. You can also store onions, garlic, sweet potatoes, and pumpkin in this way.

Tomatoes

Nobody likes a soggy tomato in their salad! Tomatoes taste amazing when they are fresh as they can be. Store them at room temperature, away from the sun, so that they will ripen evenly. You can then put them in the fridge when they are ripe.

Storage Times For Vegetables

You can store vegetables like broccoli, cabbage, carrots, celery, and potatoes in a container or plastic bag and put these in the crisper of your fridge. Mushrooms last longer when you store them in a paper bag. Keep your vegetables separate from fruit in the fridge so they don't ripen too quickly.

Here is a guideline for you to use when storing different vegetables. It will help you keep an eye on what is fresh and needs replenishing.

Type of Vegetable	Location	How Long
Asparagus	Fridge	3-4 days
Beets	Fridge	2 weeks
Broccoli	Fridge	3-5 days
Brussel Sprouts	Fridge	3-5 days
Cabbage	Fridge	1 week
Carrots	Fridge	3-4 weeks
Cauliflower	Fridge	1 week
Celery	Fridge	1-2 weeks
Corn	Fridge	1-2 days

Cucumbers	Fridge	1 week
Green Beans	Fridge	3-5 days
Green Onions	Fridge	7-10 days
Lettuce	Fridge	1 week
Mushrooms	Fridge	4-7 days
Parsnips	Fridge	3-4 weeks
Peas in pods	Fridge	3-5 days
Peppers (Red and Green)	Fridge	1-2 weeks
Potatoes	Cupboard/Cool Temp	1-2 weeks/2-3 months
Spinach	Fridge	3-5 days
Squash (zucchini)	Fridge	4-5 days
Tomatoes	Cupboard	1-5 days
Onions	Cupboard	1-2 months

Storing Canned Vegetables

You can store canned vegetables for convenience as they last a very long time. Canned vegetables can last for a whopping 1-2 years. A great tip is to label the can with the date so you know how long it has been there.

You will notice some canned vegetables will have a "use by" date on them. The manufacturer recommends this date to advise how long the quality of the food will last. If you store cans properly, you can eat them after this date.

Freezing Vegetables Is A Thing

You can freeze your fresh vegetables. It is an easy and fast way to preserve nutrients in the vegetables and have summer vegetables throughout the year. **You will need to blanch the vegetables before you freeze them.**

- Boil the vegetables either whole or cut up for 1-2 minutes.
- Next, transfer the vegetables immediately into ice-cold water.

- This process stops the cooking process and prevents freezer burn.
- Your frozen vegetables will last for up to 1 year in the freezer.

Freezing is great for making your vegetables last longer. There are some vegetables you should not freeze. These are artichokes, eggplants, endives, lettuce, potatoes (apart from mashed), radishes, sprouts, and sweet potatoes.

The Best Way To Preserve Fresh Meat

Preserving fresh meat is crucial to ensure you do not eat anything that will make you ill. Eating raw meat is dangerous, but you also want to get the most from the fresh meat you buy. Thankfully, it is easy to preserve fresh meat safely.

Preserving Fresh Meat In The Refrigerator

Putting your fresh meat in the refrigerator is the easiest way to store fresh meat. It can last for up to 6-7 days in the fridge. The duration depends on the cut of the meat, the packaging, and how fresh the meat is.

Here are some simple tips to follow to ensure your meat is as fresh as it can be in the fridge:

- ★ Don't store the meat in the package you bought it in. Take it out from the plastic, dry it with a paper towel, and put it in a rigid plastic or glass container.
- ★ Put the meat in the lower compartment of your refrigerator. The colder temperature in this area ensures less multiplication of bacteria in the meat.
- ★ Whenever you want to use meat in one of your recipes, take it out of the fridge 30 minutes before you start cooking it.

★ You might have checked it already. However, before you start cooking, check for any bad smells if it is too dry or has grey or greenish streaks.

Preserving Fresh Meat In The Freezer

Meat is expensive, and you can only use some of it in one go. If you put the meat into the freezer, you can keep it even longer. After checking that the meat is still fresh, you can do the following to store it in the freezer:

- Remove the meat from the packaging and dab it down with a paper towel to remove any liquids and juices. It then needs to go in a special container.
- You can use a glass container, an airtight sealed plastic container, or a freezing bag. Alternatively, you can wrap it several times with plastic film.
- Remember to place a label on the container showing the date you put the meat into the freezer.

Never Do This When You Are Preserving Meat

Some little mistakes can destroy the preservation process in the refrigerator or the freezer. Here are some tips to help avoid the mistakes, so you don't have to throw any expensive meat away.

★ Remember never to put fresh meat in contact with any cooked meat. There is a danger that raw food bacteria can contaminate cooked food.
★ As mentioned, always use a proper container, bag, or plastic film to cover the meat. A random plastic carrier bag will not work.
★ When you want to use some frozen meat from the freezer, take it out for at least 12 hours before using it. Let it defrost slowly in the fridge.

Preservation Times For Meat

The preservation times for meat depend on its origin and how they are processed. These factors can affect how long you can preserve the meat. Here is a quick reference guide for some common types of meat:

- **Minced meat** - must be consumed within 24 hours of buying it.
- **Veal** - will last 5 days in the refrigerator and up to 12 months in the freezer. Store it in a vacuum or frost bag.
- **Turkey or chicken (white meat)** - no more than 2-3 days in the fridge. It can last up to 6 months in the freezer if it is in vacuum or airtight containers.
- **Beef** - can stay in the fridge for 2 days and up to 12 months in the freezer. The temperature should always be -18°C.

Further Tips For Freezing Meat, Poultry, And Fish

Because fish, meat, and poultry can go off quickly. There are "sell by" dates on these food items. These expiration dates inform the grocery store how long they can display the food. Always purchase the item before the date on the package. (NB There is a more detailed section on expiration dates coming up).

Generally, always store your meat, poultry, and fish in your refrigerator at 40° F or below this temperature. If you plan on keeping it longer, you can put it in the freezer at 0° F or below this temperature. When you take something out of the freezer, you should always cook it within one or two days after defrosting.

When you freeze things properly, you can keep them for a long time. However, the food quality will decline over time if you store them longer in the freezer. Although it takes longer, always defrost fish, meat, and poultry in your fridge, instead of on your kitchen counter. Get rid of something if it has a strange color, smell, or freezer burn.

How To Store Fruit

Keeping fruit fresh can make the difference between having a crunchy, tasty snack and putting something in the garbage.

Using The Fridge To Store Fruit

If you store fruit in the fridge, it can help to make them last longer. In the fridge, you can store fruit such as apples, berries, and grapes. It's best to keep them in their original containers for extra crispiness. You can use plastic bags with tiny holes can help fruit last longer. These are perfect for releasing moisture.

Ripen Your Fruit On The Counter

Some fruit must ripen on the counter before you put it in the fridge. Examples are avocados, apricots, bananas, melons, peaches, and plums. Once they are ripe, you can transfer them to the fridge.

Fruit Storage Times For The Fridge

Here are some recommended fruit storage times for the fridge to help you:

Type of Fruit	Storage Time
Apples	3-4 weeks
Apricots	4-5 days
Avocado	3-5 days
Blueberries	1-2 weeks
Cherries	4-7 days

Cranberries	3-4 weeks
Gooseberries	2-3 days
Grapefruit	2-3 weeks
Grapes	5-7 days
Guava	3-4 days
Kiwi	5-7 days
Mango	5-7 days
Melons	7-10 days
Nectarine	3-5 days
Oranges	2-3 weeks
Pear	5-7 days
Pineapple	3-5 days
Plums	3-5 days
Pomegranate	1-2 months
Prickly pear	1-3 days
Raspberries	2-3 days
Rhubarb	5-7 days
Strawberries	3-5 days
Watermelon	2 weeks

Is Storing Fruit In A Root Cellar An Option?

It is possible to store fruit in a root cellar (if you or your family have one). For example, you can store apples in a cool, dark place for up to six months. It all depends on the humidity and temperature inside the root cellar.

Freeze Fruit To Eat Later

You don't have to overdo it and eat all your fruit at the same time. You can freeze nearly all fruit, which means you can eat it all year. Fruit normally lasts in a freezer for up to 1 year. Frozen fruit is great to mix in yogurt or to make fruit smoothies.

How To Freeze Fruit Properly

There are several ways to freeze fruit. For example, you can freeze them in small pieces while they are still whole or put them in a jar with some syrup. You can freeze berries using this method:

- ★ Wash the berries thoroughly with water and drain them.
- ★ Put the berries in a single layer on a cookie sheet.
- ★ Place them in the freezer.
- ★ You can then put them in freezer bags or containers when they are hard.

How Long Can You Store Canned Fruit?

Like canned vegetables, you can store canned fruit for up to 1-2 years. It's a great way to have a ready supply of fruit in your home. If you put a label on the can, you will know how long it has been in your cupboard.

Tip To Ripen Fruit Quicker

Sometimes, you might have some fruit that is taking time to ripen. You can speed up the process by putting the fruit into a paper bag alongside an apple or banana. These two fruit release a gas that can help other fruit to ripen.

How To Read Expiration Dates

You might not believe it, but eating food after expiration is usually safe. The expiration dates refer to quality rather than safety. According to the US Department of Agriculture's (USDA) Food Safety and Inspection Service, food products are safe to consume after expiration.

The Meaning Of Different Expiration Dates

Read this list of the different expiration dates to help you keep your food longer than before.

Best If Used By/Before

This date type relates to the quality of the food item. It is put there as a suggestion to have the food at its peak quality and taste. It is not a purchase or safety date.

Use By

This date is also a suggestion of when you should eat the food. If it is a day or two after this date, you shouldn't throw it away. You can still assess the food and then decide. (NB. It is only a safety date when used for infant formula).

Sell By

This type of date is for retailers. It helps retailers decide how long they will keep it on the shelf in the store. According to the Institute of Food Technologists, "one-third of a food's shelf-life remains after the sell-by date for the consumer to use at home."

Freeze By

The USDA states that the freeze-by date indicates when you should freeze a product to maintain its peak quality. It is not an indicator of the quality or safety date of the food.

How Long Do Foods Last After The Expiration Date?

All foods are different. The same can be said when dealing with expiration dates. Here is a list of common food items and how long they last after expiry dates.

Food Item	How Long They Last After The Expiration Date
Butter	Fridge - within 3 months Freezer - within 6 months
Cold Cuts	Fridge - 2 weeks unopened or 5 days opened Freezer - 2 months
Eggs	Fridge - within 3-5 weeks
Jams and Jellies	Fridge - 6 months opened Pantry - 1-year unopened
Ketchup	Fridge - 6 months opened Pantry - 1-year unopened
Mayonnaise	Fridge - 2 months opened Pantry - 3 months
Milk	Fridge - within 1 week Freezer - 3 months
Rice and Dried Pasta	Within 2 years
Soda	Fridge - 2 days if open Pantry - 6 months
Yoghurt	Fridge - 2 weeks Freezer - 2 months

How Long Can I Use Leftovers?

According to USDA, leftovers can last 4 days in the refrigerator. However, if the dish contains uncooked ingredients like mayonnaise or has seafood, it should be eaten in 2 days. Never leave uneaten food on a counter for more than 2 hours. The longer you leave it, the more bacteria can grow on it.

It is fine to put warm food into a refrigerator or freezer if you have a dish that might take a long time to cool down completely. The best thing is to transfer it to several small containers. Leftovers in the freezer should only stay for 3-4 months. Any longer, they become icy and absorb smells from other food in the freezer.

How To Ensure You Have Cooking Success

You don't have to be Gordon Ramsey to be a good cook. It's all about taking it easy and working with what you have. Over time your cooking skills will improve, as any skill does in life with regular practice. Here are some tips to help you achieve cooking success, so you can continue your cooking journey without stress.

Start With What You Want

You're not living with your parents now, so you are in charge of what you will eat. **Don't be scared by this. It is a liberating experience.** Think about what you would like to eat. For example, if pasta is your favorite food, start learning pasta dishes. If you like eating burgers, learn how to make one from scratch.

Keep It Simple In The Beginning

You may not be ready yet to showcase your food with confidence but everyone has to start somewhere, so don't put yourself under any pressure. You don't need to be creating 5-star Michelin restaurant quality food. Aim for creating meals that take you 30 minutes max during weeknights.

Batch Cook Your Way To Quantity

An ideal way to save time and money is to batch cook your food. Make huge portions of casserole, chilli, or lasagna dishes. You can keep some extra portions in the fridge and freeze some for a later date. Perfect for those days when you don't have much time to cook.

Start Doing Some Intuitive Cooking

Nothing is in stone. Start learning to use your instincts when you cook. Test the food as you go along and if you think it needs more salt, garlic, etc., do it! You are on your own now and don't need permission to try new things. Before you know it, you will better understand what spices and seasonings go with what.

Enjoy It!

Probably the most important point, cooking is not a serious thing. You can have fun with it while you are cooking a meal. Put on some of your favorite tunes, dance away, or invite friends over to cook with you. Once you get into cooking, you'll find it is not as scary as you thought. Use it to destress and balance yourself.

Summary

After reading this chapter, you now have the confidence to grocery shop by yourself, only if you apply what you have learned that is. You also know how to properly store all types of food, saving you time and money. Hopefully, you have already tried some of the recipes in this book and will be planning your first dinner party to show your cooking skills.

The next chapter has tips on how to deal with common home and road emergencies. Next time something happens to you, you won't need to call your parents or somebody else to help you. These skills will help you deal with problems more calmly and efficiently. Become more street-smart and have more control!

02

SURVIVING EMERGENCIES: ESSENTIAL SKILLS FOR THE HOME, ROAD & STREET SAFETY

"When you're in a tough situation, it's easy to get overwhelmed, but if you keep a level head and take one step at a time, you'll be surprised at what you can accomplish."

—BEAR GRYLLS

Becoming street-wise can lift your life to another level. You can walk with your head high, knowing you can handle practically anything. You won't need to rely on anybody else when emergencies arise. That's because you will be the person that will step into action and be there to help out.

You are the new superhero in town.

According to the WHO (World Health Organization), the leading causes of death

for young adults are accidents and injuries. It is a no-brainer that if you want to stay safe, you must know what to do in an emergency. Sadly, home and road emergencies happen, but preparing yourself to handle these situations can help.

When you have the life skills to handle any emergency, it will help you to stay calm and react in the best way possible. Next time an accident happens, you will be confident to take control and act. You won't have to call or rely on your parents or other adults. You can grab the bull by the horns and get going.

Life skills can build your confidence.

This confidence can spread to other areas of your life as you realize what you can do. It's like a new level of maturity that will swell your chest with pride. This newfound confidence will also impress your parents and those around you. You'll take more significant steps into your adult life and embrace everything.

Emergency put everything into perspective.

My nephews and nieces were always getting into trouble when they were younger. Not because they were doing something wrong but because they didn't know what to do. My siblings and I were always there to give them advice. I always made a point of advising them when they specifically asked for it. I still do. At times even when they didn't ask but that's just how I am.

Giving advice and telling somebody what to do are two different things.

Knowing what to do in a critical situation is some of the most vital advice you will ever learn. In extreme circumstances, it could be the difference between life and death. Read on to find out what to do when an emergency happens outside or inside your home. You could save your life or even somebody else's life.

How To Handle 10 Common Home Emergencies

There are so many things that can go wrong in your home. Here are the top ten home emergencies that can happen and tips on how you can handle them.

1. Taking The Heat Out Of Kitchen Fires

Kitchen fires are savage, dangerous, and difficult to control. Follow these essential tips to take control of your kitchen:

- Kitchen fires tend to start when the cook is not paying attention. Therefore, never leave your oven or stovetop when you are cooking.
- Always make a point of cooking at the time when you don't need to leave the kitchen area. It will stop you from tempting fate.
- Regularly check your smoke detectors. Set a monthly reminder to test smoke detectors and replace batteries immediately if you need to.
- You can also replace the whole smoke detector every ten years, so you can be sure that it is working correctly.

Now you know how to prevent a kitchen fire. What should you do if one starts in your kitchen? Follow these steps:

- ★ Smother a small grease fire with baking soda or slide a metal lid onto the pan to stop the fire. Also, don't forget to turn off the stove.

- ★ Never put water onto a grease fire to put it out. It is a dangerous thing to do and could make the fire even worse.
- ★ If you have an oven fire, make sure you keep the oven door closed. Also, remember to turn the oven off.
- ★ If you have followed the instructions above and the fire is still going, get everybody out of the house. Close the door and call 911 from a safe distance.

2. Stopping A Water Leak

A water leak can be as scary as a fire. Anything that you are not in control of is. Remember that the main water valve controls water flow into your home.

- One of the first things you can do when you move into your new home is to locate the main water valve (generally in the basement or at the front of a property). If in doubt ask your landlord.
- Learn how to turn this valve off in an emergency to prevent water damage to your property.
- Once you have turned the water valve off, you can call a plumber to assist you in solving the problem.

Another thing that could happen is a water leak from your ceiling. You'll need to minimize the damage as much as possible. You can do this by:

- ★ Place buckets or plastic sheets under the leak to prevent further water damage.
- ★ Have a good look around your home and see if you can find the source of the leak.
- ★ If it is a roofing problem, it is best to call a professional roofing company as soon as possible. The company can assess the damage and help with repairs.

Top Tip

This tip is ideal if you live in an area prone to cold snaps. You can insulate the pipes before the weather gets colder to stop them from freezing or bursting.

3. Managing Water Overflows

It's easy to forget, but anything containing a lot of water could overflow. Here are some tips on how to handle a toilet overflow:

- If the toilet overflows, you need to find the valve behind the toilet on the wall. You can then turn it off to stop the flow of the water.
- You then get a mop and bucket and remove any standing water. Do this quickly to limit any water damage.
- Now you can try and determine the problem. Look at the fill tube and the float. Also, check for any blockages that might stop the toilet from draining.
- If you still cannot fix the problem, you will need to call a plumber so they can come out and help you.

Also, here are some tips to help you act quickly if a bathtub or sink overflows in your home:

- If your bathtub or sink overflows, the first thing you should do is stop the water from flowing.
- You should turn the faucet off. However, if the faucet doesn't work, you must turn the main water valve off to your property.
- Like a toilet overflow, grab a mop and bucket and quickly remove any standing water.
- Finally, remember to repair the faucet before you use the bath or sink again. You don't want to have to deal with it all over again.

4. Dealing With A Flooded Basement

Remember that you should **never enter a basement if there is a flood**. It is perilous to do so. These are the best steps to take in this situation:

- Follow health and safety protocols by calling your utility companies. Stay away from the basement until the professionals turn the electricity and gas off.
- Hire a professional to help you clean up the mess to reduce the damage and help prevent any potential health problems.
- It's also important to throw out anything that the flood water touched unless it can be cleaned and disinfected.

5. What To Do In A Power Outage Situation

There's nothing worse than watching your favorite movie or series and having a power outage. It can be frustrating and a little worrying when you go into darkness.

While you might not be able to prevent a power outage, you can follow these steps when it does happen:

- Check outside to see if other homes and streetlights have power during the outage.
- If the lights outside are still on, you will need to check the circuit breakers in your home.
- If the lights outside are off, you can call the power company. Alternatively, go to their website to report it and ask for the repair time.

It's important to stay safe when there is a power outage. Follow these steps to make sure you are safe and secure:

- ★ The safest thing to do is use a flashlight in the home instead of lighting some candles.
- ★ Keep your flashlights in an easy-to-find location that you will remember. Test the flashlights monthly and keep spare batteries nearby.
- ★ Alternatively, you can use the torch from your mobile to help you walk around your home.
- ★ Don't be tempted to open up the refrigerator. Food can go off in the fridge when the power has been off for four hours, so keep it closed.
- ★ Turn off any lights that were on when the power went off. Also, unplug electrical items that were on during the outage.

Top Tip

Invest in a small generator if you live in an area with power outage issues that can last several days. It can provide electricity for a refrigerator or freezer.

6. Preventing Carbon Monoxide Poisoning

Carbon monoxide is a clear, odorless gas that can cause severe illness or even death. If you suffer from carbon monoxide poisoning, it can feel like the flu without the fever. If you think you are suffering from this, **you must call 911 immediately.**

Here are some things you can do to prevent carbon monoxide poisoning:

- Start using carbon monoxide detectors. Test them monthly to make sure they are working well. Replace them according to the manufacturer's instructions.
- Make an important note in your diary to have all your gas appliances checked at least once every year.

- Ensure all your gas appliances have proper ventilation, such as fireplaces, gas furnaces, and water heaters.
- Don't get complacent using gas-powered appliances. Always follow the safety instructions when using space heaters and generators, etc.

7. How To Handle A Gas Leak

Luckily, most people can smell a natural gas leak. It can smell like rotten eggs or sulfur. Leaks don't happen that often, but you have to act straight away when they do. A leak inside your home can make you ill and cause an explosion.

If you notice the smell of natural gas when you are inside your home, follow these steps:

- Go outside of your home **IMMEDIATELY.** Call the utility company and 911.
- Do not go and look for the leak yourself.
- Do not touch switches for any electrical appliances. Leave them alone.
- Do not smoke a cigarette or have any open flames in your home.

8. What To Do When You Have Broken Glass

Grabbing a dustpan and brush might come to mind when dealing with broken glass. But it is more complex than that. Here's how to handle glass safely:

- **Never handle glass with bare hands.** Before you do anything, put on a pair of thick or rubber gloves.
- Use a piece of cardboard or some stiff paper to remove the large pieces of glass. Use large duct tape to help pick up the little bits of glass.

- After you have removed the glass, if the area is still wet, you can use a mop or paper towels to dry everything.
- If the glass broke on a carpet, vacuum the area thoroughly with the hose attachment.
- If the broken glass is from a window pane, seal the area temporarily with a trash bag cut to size. Tape several layers of this to the window with duct tape.
- Call a glazing company to schedule a repair or a new window replacement, depending on the problem.

9. What To Do When Your HVAC Stops Working

When you have problems with your heating or air conditioning, the best thing to do is to call a proper technician. The technician can inspect it and decide whether it can be repaired or needs to be completely new.

When air-conditioning breaks in the warmer months, it can be problematic to stay cool. Here are some things you can do to maintain a proper body temperature, prevent heat stroke and feel cooler.

- Drink more ice water and avoid drinking alcohol because it can raise your body temperature.
- Look after your digestion by eating easy fruits and vegetables for your body to digest.
- Use a washcloth and rinse it under cold water. You can then put it on your wrists, neck, and behind your knees to keep your body cool.
- Because heat rises, you can temporarily sleep downstairs. It will make it easier for you to sleep at night.

On the flip side, if your furnace breaks down during the colder months, you must find ways to stay safe and warm. Here are some tips to help you:

- ★ Put on different layers of clothing. You can take clothes off or put them on depending on your body temperature.
- ★ **Don't use your oven to stay warm.** Heating your home like this is dangerous and will cost you money.
- ★ Heat a small area in your home with a fireplace or space heater. Only use these types of heating when you are awake, and check your ventilation.
- ★ Hang up bedspreads, curtains, and quilts over doors and windows to retain the heat. (Keep one or two free for ventilation if you use a fire).

10. Dealing With An Ant or Rodent Infestation

Creating a cozy home is nice, but you don't want to share it with unwanted guests! If you notice ants or rodents in your home, it's time to take action. Follow these steps to stay ant and rodent free:

- If you find a trail of ants in your home, remove them straight away. Clean the trail with vinegar spray to remove the ant scents.
- Look for any cracks or gaps near doors, floorboards, and windows. Set up ant traps in these areas.
- If the problem persists, you can call an expert to come in and check if there is an ant nest near your home.
- **NB If the ants are large, black carpenter ants, it is best to call a professional to deal with the problem as soon as possible.**

When a mouse or rat decides to invade your home, you can follow these tips to fix the problem:

- The first time you spot a rodent, walk around your house inside and out. Look for signs of rodent activity, such as chewing, droppings, or nests.

- Look for small holes or crevices where the rodent might have entered your home.
- If you find some entry points, you can easily cover them with sealant or wire mesh.
- Set up some rodent traps in the problem areas. If the issue persists, you need to call an expert to fix the problem.

What To Do If You Are Alone And Start Choking

Imagine eating your favorite meal you cooked and sitting in your lovely, cozy home all by yourself. You are all relaxed and enjoying the moment when suddenly you start choking on some food. **What should you do next?**

Being by yourself in such a situation is frightening. You might not have met the neighbors yet and don't fancy knocking on their door for help.

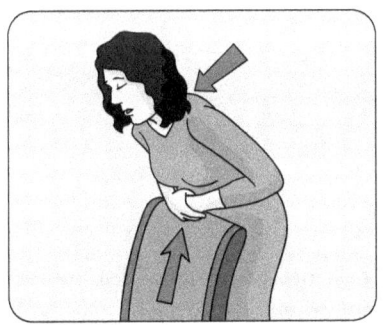

Would you have time to even get to your neighbors anyway? **You need to act fast!**

You must perform the **Heimlich Maneuver** on yourself, so you don't choke to death. Knowing how to do this could help to save your life one day. Follow these steps to unblock your obstruction.

- Conscious choking is when you cannot breathe, cough, cry, or speak. **The first thing you should do is dial 911.**
- It doesn't matter if you can't talk. 911 operators can usually trace the call and will send help on its way before you lose consciousness.
- Next, find something like a chair or kitchen countertop. Then repeatedly thrust your abdomen on it to dislodge the stuck object.

- Remember to keep thrusting until the object dislodges in your body. You can pick up the phone and talk to the operator when the obstruction is free.
- **If pregnant, make a fist with your hands above your baby bump. Thrust the fist into your body until the object is free.**

Hopefully, you will never have to experience this. But there are things you can do to prevent it from happening to you in the first place.

- ★ Cut your food into small pieces before you eat it. It's not a "babyish" thing to do. Remember, it could save your life.
- ★ Eat your food slowly and chew your food correctly. It doesn't matter if it takes you longer to eat your meal. It will make it easier for you to digest.
- ★ Always remember to eat food when you are sitting upright. Eating food while laying makes it difficult for the food to move around your body.
- ★ Drink water with your meal.

What Can You Do To Help If Someone Is Choking

If you notice somebody you are with is choking, you might have to step in to help them. When somebody is choking, it cuts off oxygen to their brain, and giving first aid can help to save their life.

- Firstly, you will need to assess the situation. If the person can cough, let them cough, as it may help to dislodge the stuck object.
- If you notice that the person cannot cough, cry, laugh, or talk, you will need to give first aid to the person.
- The best thing to do first is to give **five back blows.**

How To Give Back Blows

- ★ You can do this by standing at the side behind the choking person. Put your arm across the person's chest to support the body.
- ★ Then bend the person over. You can do this at their waist so they are facing the floor.
- ★ Use the heel of your hand to hit five times between the person's shoulder blades.
- ★ If this doesn't work, you will need to give the person **five abdominal thrusts** via the **Heimlich Maneuver**.

How To Give Abdominal Thrusts

- ★ To do the Heimlich Maneuver, you must stand behind the choking person. Place one foot slightly in front of your other for balance.
- ★ Wrap your arms around the waist and tip the person forward slightly. Make a fist with one hand and put it above the belly button.
- ★ Grab your fist with your other hand and press into the person's stomach in a quick upward motion. Almost as if you will lift them.
- ★ Do this five times and check to see if the blockage has come free. **If it hasn't worked, alternate between five blows and five thrusts.**

Top Tip

It's worth taking a first aid course. You might have to pay for one, but many options are available on the market. Alternatively, you could download a first aid app on your phone. These apps allow you to access information within as little as 30 seconds. You can also check out online videos to further your understanding.

How To Handle 10 Common Road Emergencies

You now know how to handle the most common emergencies in the home. It's not only in the home where things can go wrong. Many emergencies can happen outside as well. You might be the world's most safe and most cautious driver. But accidents can happen when you drive, and you'll need to act fast.

If you don't drive, save yourself some time and move on to the next section of the book, "How to become street-wise." If you drive, read on to learn about ten of the most common road emergencies and tips on handling them so you can stay safe and secure.

1. What To Do When You Have A Tire Blowout

Thankfully, tire blowouts are not as common as they used to be years ago. However, they still happen, and your quick reactions can help save your life. Follow these three tips if you are driving and your tire suddenly goes flat.

- Immediately hold the steering wheel as hard as possible and keep the car driving straight. It will feel harder to control, but staying in your lane on the road is essential. **Put on your four-way flashlights to alert other drivers that something is wrong.**
- Slow down gradually. Take your foot off the gas pedal and let the car slow down. **Don't use any brakes until the car has nearly stopped.** You might automatically feel like you want to brake, but doing that could cause you to spin or even crash.
- Try not to stop on the road if possible. Doing so puts you in danger from other cars hitting you. Once you have slowed down and are in control of the vehicle, pull off the road in a safe place. You can then replace the tire or call somebody to help you.

2. How To Stay Safe When Your Headlights Are Not Working

Many things can go wrong when you are driving. Losing your lights can be scary and dangerous, as it plunges you straight into darkness. Follow these quick steps to handle the situation as best as you can.

- If your headlights stop working, **instantly try your four-way flashlights, parking lights, and directional signal lights.**
- These lights should still work and can help you see to get off the road safely. Also, other drivers will be aware that you have a problem.
- If you notice that your headlights are getting dimmer, take immediate action. Drive to the nearest service station, or pull over and see if you can fix the issue. If not, then take it to your nearest mechanic to investigate. You may think you can get by but it could end up causing you issues when you need the headlights the most - like driving back from a party at 2 am through some country lanes where there are no streetlights. Okay, maybe a bit of an extreme example but I only want to stress the importance of the point.

3. How To Act When Your Accelerator/Throttle Is Stuck

You've probably realized that when a problem happens, the priority is to stay in control of the vehicle. The same applies if you encounter a problem with your accelerator/throttle.

- If your accelerator/throttle appears stuck, you can try lifting it with your big toe. **Under no circumstance take your eyes off the road or reach down with your hand.**
- **Turn on your emergency four-way flashes** to let other drivers know you have a problem. If you cannot lift the pedal with your toe, try tapping it several times to see if that releases it.

- When that doesn't work, **shift to neutral and apply the brakes.** The engine will race ahead, but the brakes will slow the car down. Put the brakes down firmly but don't pump them. Move off the road when you can.
- **Do not turn the engine off to stop the car from moving unless you have no choice.** If you do this, it will affect the steering and power-assist braking system. The vehicle will then be harder to control.
- When the car comes to a stop, you can then turn off the ignition. If you have an on/off switch, hold that down till it turns off. If you have a key, you must keep it in the ignition to stop the sterling wheel from locking.

4. Staying Calm When Your Brakes Don't Work

This scenario is the worst thing that can happen when driving. It's not like in cartoons or a movie. It could be a traumatic real-life situation for you. You must stay calm and follow these steps to protect yourself if it happens.

- **Immediately reduce your speed.** If you have an automatic car, try the brakes again and pump them if you have to. Newer cars have dual braking systems, which means a backup will take over and give you some braking power. If you have a manual transmission, move down into a lower gear.
- **Turn on four-way emergency flashers** to notify other drivers and **apply the emergency brake.** You can do this by pressing the button and gradually pulling the emergency brake into the off position. NB This might cause the back wheels to lock, and you might skid, be prepared.
- Look around for an **uphill slope** and drive towards it. It will help you to **decelerate** more. If you are still having trouble and need to hit something, **choose the softest thing you can see.**

- Don't be tempted to turn off the ignition while driving. Doing this could affect your ability to maneuver the car safely and worsen your situation.

5. Your Engine Stalls Or Doesn't Work At All

There are many different reasons your engine might stall or not work. **Regularly maintaining your car** can prevent many things, like overheating, running out of gas, and not having enough oil.

However, other problems might surprise you when you are out on the road. You could have a transmission failure, problems with the catalytic converter or ignition system, electrical issues, or a faulty fuel pump.

If you have an issue with one of these problems:

- **Turn on your four-way emergency flashes** and get the vehicle safely off the road as soon as possible.
- If your car has completely shut down and steering it or braking are the issues, you can follow the advice earlier in this chapter.
- Once your vehicle is off the road, put it into neutral gear and try to restart the engine.
- If you can get the car to start, return to the road and go off the next exit if you are on a limited-access highway. If you are in a town, go to a repair shop.

6. You Are About To Hit Another Car

When you are about to collide with a car, you must act fast in a life-or-death situation. But do you know how to quickly stop or drive around a major incident on the highway? Read on to find out.

- If you have ABS, you can turn your vehicle while braking and have less or no skidding. **It's important not to jerk the steering wheel,** as the system will push you further.
- Use ABS in a parking lot to get a feel for how it works.
- If you don't have ABS, step on the brake pedal, and stop turning the steering wheel. Braking will slow the car, putting more weight on the front tires and allowing you to turn quicker.

Remember that it is best to run the car off the road than crash head-on into another moving object. Try to keep your vehicle as straight as possible, so you can control your turn and not drive into traffic.

7. Avoiding The Local Wildlife

It's nice to see nature in the wild, but it can be a potential disaster when it runs in front of your car! Depending on where you live, you might bump into a bear, deer, or moose. Collisions can happen anytime, so you must be on your guard.

- Pay close attention when driving and constantly scan the road, especially in remote areas.
- **Use your headlight beams when you can.** You can also reduce your speed in known wild animal areas so you have more time to react.
- Deer move as a family unit, and coyotes and wolves move in packs. If you dodge one animal, there might be more!
- **If you've seen one animal, apply your brakes.** You can brake as though preparing for a collision and try to stay in your lane.

8. You Accidently Drive Off The Road

You might think you would never drive off the road. But it can happen if you are tired or distracted while driving. It is also possible when there is bad weather or poor visibility.

- **Don't make a knee-jerk reaction!** You might try to overcompensate, cross the line into oncoming traffic and cause an accident.
- Removing your foot from **the accelerator** and gently putting the wheels back onto the road is best. Then lightly applying the brakes if you need to.
- If you drove off the road because you were tired, pull over as soon as possible and take a break.

9. You Hit Severe Weather Or Start Hydroplaning

It's always good to check the weather report before you head out in the car. Even more so if it is the time of year for storms or you will drive in a storm-prone area. Knowing the different definitions and guidelines can help you prepare.

- **Significant Weather Advisory** - This advisory is given to the public to advise that the weather is dangerous but not life-threatening. The weather could involve excessive lightning, hail smaller than 1" in diameter, heavy rain, or winds up to 58mph.
- **Severe Thunderstorm Warning** - This radar warning indicates that things have been noted or are near the specific warned area. It is a danger alert and has a risk of becoming a tornado. There could be cloud-to-ground lightning, some hail of 1" or more, and wind greater than 58mph.
- **Tornado Watch** - As the name suggests, a tornado could be on your horizon! The warning means the conditions are favorable for a tornado to develop. The public should monitor the conditions and take action to avoid the tornado if the weather worsens.
- **Tornado Warning** - The next thing up from Tornado Watch is a Tornado Warning. It means a twister is developing on the radar or is already on the ground. Never try to outrun a tornado. **You should abandon your vehicle straight away.** Seek shelter in a ditch or a sturdy structure.

There is another danger you might face from heavy rain or storms, and that is hydroplaning. **It can occur when you travel more than 35mph and the rain is heavy enough for the car to ride across the water.**

It's important to note that the faster you drive, the harder it is for your tires to push the water aside. The more water there is, the harder it is for you to control your car. Hydroplaning is one of the leading causes of accidents during bad weather.

- Monitor your tire tread and ensure that your tires are always correctly inflated.
- Always slow down when it rains, and avoid driving through standing water.
- If you hydroplane, take your foot off the accelerator and let the car slow down gradually.
- Apply the non-ABS brakes by slowly pumping them. Or, for ABS brakes, you can brake gently.

10. You Have To Drive On Icy Roads

Winter driving conditions can be brutal. It's best to avoid driving in these conditions if you can. When you start skidding on ice, it's easy to start panicking and worsening the situation. It's best to keep a calm, level head to deal with the issue.

Most accidents happen when drivers try to get their tires to do more than they can in dangerous conditions. For example, spinouts and uncontrolled slides can occur when a driver steers while braking or turns while accelerating.

- You can avoid risky situations by coming to a stop before turning the wheel to go around a corner.
- You can apply consistent but light pressure to the throttle if you have to turn from a complete stop.

- If you slide, take your foot off the accelerator and lightly turn into the slide. Turning against the slide will cause an aggressive slide the other way.
- Don't hit your brakes, as this will make your tail end slip out even further than it was.

How To Become Street-Wise

Young adults are affected by crime more than any other age group. Becoming more street-wise can help you stay safe and not be another victim of crime. Here are ten tips to help you stay more vigilant when you are out and about.

1) It doesn't matter where you are or what you are doing. You could be driving, at school, the mall, waiting for a bus or subway, or out on the street. Always make sure you are alert and stay tuned into your surroundings. **Treat everywhere with the same degree of caution.**
2) If you are in an area, you don't know. **Always come across as calm and confident and give the message that you know where you are going.**
3) Don't walk through alleys and parking lots. Also, don't take short-cuts or walk in wooded areas. Also, stick to well-lighted, traveled streets.
4) **Never accept a gift or a ride from somebody you don't know or you don't trust.** The same also applies to somebody you have just met on the internet. People can pretend to be somebody else on the internet, and you might have problems meeting them in person.
5) Keep in mind the area where you live, go to school, or work. Get to know all the locations of the fire stations, police stations, and public telephones in case you need to go to one. **It's also good to know which restaurants and stores stay open late.**

6) When you walk to and from your friend's houses, go to school or the stores. **Always take the safest route there and back.** Have a backup plan, so if you encounter a problem, you know where to get some help without thinking twice.
7) Don't show off your cash or anything else that looks expensive or involves money. Cell phones, expensive jewelry, and clothing can grab attention and make you a target for a potential robbery. **Keep these items out of sight.**
8) If you like to use a backpack or purse, keep them close to your body and always close them. If you prefer to use a wallet, put it inside your coat or in your front pants pocket. **Make sure to put your wallet in your front pocket or a backpack.**
9) **Remember to keep your car or house key in your hand before you reach the door.** It will stop you from searching for it when you should already be inside your home.
10) **Always rely on your gut instincts.** If somebody or something makes you uncomfortable, avoid the situation or person and leave as soon as possible.

Summary

You now know how to react quickly and with confidence in emergencies. It doesn't matter if something happens to you at home or if you are out driving in your car. You won't panic because you can use your new life-saving skills to help yourself and possibly somebody else.

In the next chapter you will learn even more skills to help you daily! You can read easy tips on basic home and car repairs, and general maintenance tips to get the most from the things you own. You will learn the true meaning of "Do It Yourself" and how you can reap the maintenance benefits.

03

DIY MOVEMENT: HOME & CAR REPAIR/MAINTENANCE SKILLS

"It is the neglect of timely repair that makes rebuilding necessary."
—RICHARD WHATELY

You've decided to strike out on your own. It's liberating and character-building living by yourself. Once you've made a move, you don't want to take any steps backward. Give yourself every opportunity to learn and grow. Taking control of your life and learning basic repairs and maintenance can minimize those "Help me!" calls.

Learning is just a starting point to something greater.

In this chapter, you can quickly learn how to fix some of the essential things in your home. It will save you money from buying new things, and you'll realize that you can do more than you think! Get ready to debunk the mysteries of repair and maintenance and get fixing things! You'll learn how to do things the right way, so you'll know for next time.

It doesn't matter if you're not the most technical of people. There are many basic repairs anybody can do at home. It only takes a little bit of patience and trust to give it a go. It's not rocket science.

Sometimes You'll Have To Leave It To The Experts

Before you start, it is important to know that you won't be able to fix everything. This situation is no reflection on yourself. It is simply the fact that you are not an expert. You might learn to love it and want to do it as a career. But for now, it's best to learn the basics, do them well and stick to them.

Here are some maintenance tasks that you should leave for the experts:

- ★ Asbestos removal
- ★ Electrical rewiring
- ★ Major plumbing
- ★ Mold removal
- ★ Roofing repairs
- ★ Structural changes or major modifications
- ★ Pest infestations
- ★ Water damage

Why You Should Do DIY Home Maintenance

Home maintenance doesn't have to be boring and a waste of time. If you were thinking of skipping this chapter, it might be best to hang around. You'll find out why it is worth spending time and effort to do it. Read on to discover two reasons why you should learn DIY home maintenance.

It's All About Learning Life Skills

When you move into adulthood, you will learn many new skills daily. A world of information is yours if you want to know it. You don't need to worry about it. You need to learn it. Life skills can help you now and prepare you for the rest of your life.

You Can Enjoy Saving Money

At times, you will have to use the skills of an expert. However, experts can be expensive, and for the smaller, more basic tasks, you can save a ton of money by doing it yourself. You are doing the labor, so you won't have to pay for that. In theory, you'll only be paying for parts. Put the money you saved away and use it on a rainy day!

Home Repairs and Maintenance You Can Do

Homeowners and renters are performing these easy tasks every day in their homes. You can be one of them too and start fixing your home. You can also look at YouTube videos for further information if you can't find everything you need in this chapter. Sometimes seeing something can help reinforce what you have read.

Fixing or Replacing a Broken Toilet Lever

Toilet levers can break frequently, but luckily they are easy to fix. Firstly, you'll need to assess if it is beyond repair and needs replacing or if it is a quick fix.

- ★ If the lever doesn't flush when you press it, open the tank. You might only need to re-attach the chain inside the tank.
- ★ If the handle looks corroded, one of the parts attached to the flapper could be beyond repair.

★ You can buy a replacement toilet lever kit. You will need an adjustable wrench to help you put it in.

Unclogging a Blocked Toilet

It's maybe not the nicest of jobs! But you can unblock a toilet yourself without calling in some expensive help.

★ Try a round toilet plunger to unclog the toilet. It will make a tight seal with the drain when you start plunging.
★ If this doesn't work, try a toilet auger. A toilet auger is a long flexible tool like a drain snake. It can go down the toilet and unblock places plungers can't.
★ You can put three tablespoons of liquid dish soap into the toilet bowl before using the plunging or auger. The liquid helps to lubricate the drain.

Fixing P-Traps Under Bathroom and Kitchen Sinks

Pipe leaks happen from time to time. Before you panic, this type of leak is minor, and you can fix it. The leaks usually occur around the P-Trap. It can happen because a worn-out washer or compression nut might be broken or loose.

You can fix it by using the following tools:

- A bucket
- A 3-way plumber's wrench
- A new P-Trap or a replacement washer

You can follow these steps to repair it yourself:

- ★ Turn the water off to the sink before you do anything. You might find the valve next to the sink, or it could be in your basement.
- ★ All you have to do is twist off the compression nuts that hold the P-Trap in place. You can then replace them and any worn-out washers.

Unblocking A Jammed Garbage Disposal

The garbage disposal might freak you out because of all the blades and the noise. Don't let this put you off when you have a jam.

You can fix it by using the following tools:

- ¼ inch Allen wrench
- Garbage disposal wrench
- Flashlight
- Pliers

You can follow these steps to repair it yourself:

- ★ Hit the reset button, and sometimes this will fix it for you. If that doesn't work, you can do a couple of other things.
- ★ Use the Allen wrench to rotate the disposal blades. Doing this can dislodge debris and get it working again.
- ★ Alternatively, if the job is more challenging, you may need to use the garbage disposal wrench. The wrench is designed to go into the disposal's main chamber and can remove whatever is in there.

Replacing A Broken Light Switch

As mentioned at the start of the chapter, you should leave major electrical work to an electrician. But replacing a broken light switch is a simple task.

You can fix it by using the following tools:

- Flathead screwdriver
- Phillips head screwdriver
- Replacement light switch

You can follow these steps to repair it yourself:

★ Turn off the circuit breaker that belongs to the location of the light switch so you can fix it safely.
★ Unscrew the faceplate of the light switch and disconnect the wires.
★ Connect up the new light switch and replace the faceplate.

Patching Up Drywall Holes

Holes in walls will happen. You might have hung up a picture or accidentally banged into the wall. Whatever the reason, don't worry, as you can easily fix this.

You can fix it by using the following tools:

- Drywall
- Drywall tape
- Electric drill
- Grit sandpaper
- Putty knife
- 1" x 1" wood board
- Joint compound or spackle
- Wood screws

You can follow these steps to repair it yourself:

★ Assess the actual damage. It is easy to fix if it is a small hole. First, clean the area and wipe down the wall.

- ★ Use the putty knife to put some spackle into the hole in the wall and let it dry.
- ★ When it is dry, you can smooth the area with sandpaper.
- ★ Depending on the color, you might have to paint it a bit.
- ★ If it is a larger hole, you should cut out some of the drywall around the area and replace it.
- ★ If the hole is large and you are not confident, call in a professional who will use more advanced techniques where an electric drill and wood screws might be required.

Loosening Up A Stuck Window

Sometimes, if you haven't opened a window for a while, it can become stuck. It can be tricky to open, but it is not impossible. Try prying it open yourself, or use a bit of gentle hammering. If this doesn't work, you might need to use some chemicals.

You can fix it by using the following tools:

- Cleaning supplies
- Putty Knife
- Paint Thinner
- WD40, or you can use a "dry" silicon lubricant spray
- A Rag

You can follow these steps to repair it yourself:

- ★ Use paint thinner to help loosen a stubborn window, especially if the paint prevents it from opening.
- ★ Use WD-40 or a silicon lubricant to help make the window start sliding in its tracks again.

Top Tip

WD-40 can gum up vinyl windows, so only use a little to dissolve rust. Don't spray it all over the window tracks, as you'll have another problem on your hands and we don't want that.

Basic Car Repairs and Maintenance You Can Do Yourself

Basic car repairs and maintenance can save you a fortune in money. Anybody can do it. It doesn't matter if you are new to driving or have bought your first car. You can give your car a maintenance treat and tender the loving care it deserves. It will also give you the confidence your vehicle is safe on your next exciting road trip!

As before, if you don't drive, save yourself some time and move on to the next section in the book, "An Interactive Element Especially For You." Here you can use a home maintenance checklist to help you. If you do drive, this next section will be invaluable for you.

Treat your car like your home and give it the best attention.

Before you get to the nitty-gritty of car maintenance, look at your car's vehicle owner/service manual for your car. It will give you the crucial information you need to know about your car's service needs and mileage. When you know what these are for the model of your vehicle, you can stay on top to keep it in optimal condition.

Changing The Oil

Regularly check the oil in your car. It will make your engine run smoothly and prolong its lifespan. **Changing the oil is an essential DIY skill for**

car maintenance that anybody can do. The only exception would be your oil filter, and oil drain plug are in a difficult place to reach.

You can change the oil using these steps:

- First, drain the oil by removing the drain plug, unscrewing the oil filter, and emptying it.
- You can then put the oil filter and drain plug back into the car, remove the cap where you fill the oil, and pour in some fresh oil.

Changing A Flat Tire In 5 Easy Steps

Tires are a crucial part of the car. You must look after them to ensure your vehicle is safe and secure. Now and then, you might get a flat tire. Changing a tire is quite commonplace, but if you are in the middle of nowhere, **it could be a life-changing skill you are glad you learned!**

Change the tire by following these easy steps:

- Use a jack stand to lift the car off the ground.
- Loosen the lug nuts with a wrench and remove them.
- Then you can remove the tire.
- Put the spare tire on and use the wrench to put the lug nuts back on.
- Lower the car and do another check to make sure the lug nuts are tight.

Changing The Spark Plugs

You have probably seen spark plugs a thousand times, but what do they do? Spark plugs are tiny devices inside the cylinder that create sparks. These sparks ignite the gasoline that powers your car. Spark plugs can wear out after 10,000 miles through wear and tear.

You can change your spark plugs by:

- Locate the spark plugs in your car.
- First, remove the spark plug wire and then the faulty spark plug.
- Put in a new spark plug and put the spark plug wire back in place.

Removing Scratches From Your Paintwork

Your car is your pride and joy. There's nothing worse when you see a scratch on it. It might be small, but you can't help looking at it every time you get into the car. It can be expensive to fix in a body shop. Luckily, if it is a small scratch, you can fix it yourself and save money!

You can remove minor scratches on your car by:

- Checking how deep the scratch is on your vehicle.
- Lightly sand the scratch, clean the area and then apply rubbing compound.
- Polish the area with the rubbing compound and then wash it.
- To finish it off, wax the area to seal the repair.

How To Change A Car Battery

Car batteries can last a long time. **But sod's law, your car battery will break when you least expect it.** It all depends on when it happens. If you are in a remote area, your best bet is to use roadside assistance and wait for the tow truck to get you. On the other hand, if you are at home when it happens, you can spring into action.

You can change your car battery by:

- Remove any covers that might be on the battery.
- Disconnect the negative cables and move the clamp from the battery post.

- Do precisely the same for the positive cables and move the clamp.
- Remove all screws.
- Replace the battery with the new one and reconnect the cable clamps.

Top Tip

You can label the cables before you remove them so you don't get confused.

Replacing A Broken Headlight Or Taillight

If you have a broken headlight or taillight, you will have to replace it sooner rather than later. **Not only is it an inconvenience, but it is also illegal** and could get you in trouble. Once again, you don't need to pay for it. You can do it all yourself.

You can replace a broken headlight or taillight by:

- Removing all screws connecting the headlight or taillight frame to the bracket.
- Disconnect the electrical connector and remove the broken bulb.
- Replace the bulb with a new one and plug the connector back on.
- Finally, put the frame back into place.

Top Tip

Sometimes, you might find that only the frame is the problem. If this is the case, you can change it in the same way as detailed above.

Replacing Your Windscreen Wipers

You might think windscreen wipers are not that important to the safety of your car. However, if you are in a bad storm and they don't work. Not only would it make it difficult for you to see, but it might also damage your vehicle. **It would help if you kept an eye on the wipers so you know when to replace them.**

Replace your windscreen wipers by:

- Lifting the wiper arm at an angle away from your windshield.
- Press the small tab that lets you pull the wiper blade off.
- Line up the new wiper blade with the arm and push it in firmly.

Replacing The Air Filters

Most people forget about a vehicle's air filters. However, the air filters are a vital part of your vehicle as they help to **keep the engine free of contaminants and dust.** You don't need to worry about contacting a specialist for this. The air filters are easy to replace and don't cost much money.

You can replace your air filters by:

- Open the hood to your car and locate the air filter unit.
- Remove the air filter cover and take the air filter out.
- Clean the housing for the air filter, insert a new filter and replace the cover.

Top Tip

Changing air filters every 30,000 miles or once annually is best.

Changing Your Brake Pads

You know from earlier in the book how to brake safely during an emergency. Looking after your brake pads can also ensure you are safe in your vehicle. **If you can change a tire, you can change some brake pads**, as you need to change them in the same area.

You can change your brake pads by:

- Raise the car on a jack stand and loosening the lug nuts.
- Remove the wheels, the slider bolts, and the old brake pads.
- Put new brake pads, the slider bolts, and the wheels back on.
- Double-check that everything is on securely.

Jumpstarting Your Car

The last thing that is good to know is how to jumpstart your vehicle. It's a handy skill to learn and will save you from having to call roadside assistance if your car doesn't start. **You'll also be able to step in and help somebody else if you carry some cables in your car for emergencies.**

- Get your jumper cables ready.
- **Put both cars into neutral and turn the ignition off.**
- Attach one of the red clips to the positive terminal of your battery.
- Put the other red clip into the positive terminal in the working vehicle.
- Attach one of the black clips to the negative terminal in the car that works.
- **Attach the other black clip to an unpainted metal surface.**
- Now, try starting your car.

An Interactive Element Especially For You

Here is one of the **interactive elements** in the book. You can use the following maintenance checklist to help you stay organized in your home. You'll be able to maintain everything in advance to use at the right time of the year. It will stop you from feeling overwhelmed and will make you more productive.

Home Maintenance Checklist

The home maintenance checklist is in monthly, quarterly, biannual, and annual formats so that you can stay on top of everything. Instead of worrying about what you need to do, use this as an easy reference guide. Mark items off in the checklist below when you have done them. Use a pencil so you can reuse it every year.

Monthly

- ★ Clean the kitchen sink disposal with vinegar ice cubes.
- ★ Clean the range hood filters with a degreaser.
- ★ Inspect fire extinguishers if you have one.
- ★ Inspect and change HVAC filters, especially if you have allergies.

Quarterly

- ★ Check your water softener and add salt if necessary.
- ★ Run water and flush toilets in any unused spaces such as guest bathrooms.
- ★ Test your garage door auto-reverse feature to avoid child deaths.
- ★ Test your smoke/carbon dioxide detectors using the "test" button.

Biannually

- ★ Do a deep cleaning of your house every six months. Clean everything.
- ★ Change the batteries every six months, regardless.
- ★ Test the pressure relief valve for your water heater.
- ★ Vacuum your refrigerator coils, so they are clean and use less energy.

Annually

Spring

- ★ Check your exterior drainage - gutters and pavements.
- ★ Check trees are not affecting any power lines.
- ★ Clear away any dead plants or shrubs.
- ★ Get the air conditioning ready for the summer and have a service.
- ★ Inspect the roof for any damage or leaks.
- ★ Inspect outside the home to see if you need to paint.
- ★ Repair or replace any window screens that are damaged.

Summer

- ★ Check and clean any vents in the house, such as a dryer vent or exhaust vent.
- ★ Check and repair grout in the bathroom and kitchen.
- ★ Clean and repair (if needed) the decking/patio.
- ★ Clean out any window wells.
- ★ Clean out the garage.
- ★ Deal with any insect problems.
- ★ Inspect all the plumbing for any leaks or pressure problems.

Fall

- ★ Check the driveway and pavement for any cracks.
- ★ Buy any winter items, such as shovels and sidewalk salt, ready for the winter.
- ★ Prepare the heating system for winter and check gaps in doors/windows.
- ★ Clean the chimney ready to be used in the winter.
- ★ Test that your sump pump is working properly.
- ★ Protect air conditioning units ready for the winter.

- ★ Flush out the water heater and remove any sediment that has built up.
- ★ Turn off and flush outdoor faucets and also hose pipes.

Winter

- ★ Check the caulking around bathtubs and showers.
- ★ Check the deadbolts and locks on doors and windows.
- ★ Deep clean the basement.
- ★ Regularly check for ice dams or icicles and remove them.
- ★ Remove showerheads and get rid of any sediment that has built up.
- ★ Carefully test the electricity throughout your home.
- ★ Tighten any handles and knobs that are loose.

Chapter Three Summary

After this chapter, you will know how to carry out essential maintenance and repairs in your home and car. These valuable skills will last a lifetime, and you can always share your new knowledge with family and friends. The last two chapters showed you that there are many things you can do yourself quite easily.

In the next chapter, I'll be putting the spotlight on you! I'll explain the link between your mental and physical health. You'll find out what you can do to ensure your well-being, keeping your mind and body in the best shape possible. It will help you keep growing as a person and help you to excel in life!

04

PRIORITY NUMERO UNO: TAKING CARE OF YOUR MENTAL & PHYSICAL HEALTH

"You don't have to control your thoughts. You just have to stop letting them control you."

—DAN MILLMAN

Your mental and physical health are paramount regardless of how old you are. However, as a young adult, what influences you now, could affect you for the rest of your life. You don't need to wait till you are older. You can take the proper steps to look after yourself and create a happy, positive future.

Every word and thought can affect your health and well-being.

Whatever you think and feel will affect you internally. You might be experiencing stress in your current career or studies. Without realizing it, all this stress can affect your physical and mental health. It can make you feel stuck in life and demotivate you. These feelings stop you from achieving what you want in life.

Look after your mental and physical health to create a better life.

This chapter will explain the intricate connection between your physical and mental health. You will learn how to improve your well-being by eating the right food and exercising. You'll also learn some easy mindfulness exercises you can do daily to help you stay calm and grounded.

Because this chapter is so important, you will find it is one of the longest in the book. Your wellness is one of the most vital things in your life. If you are mentally and physically well, it can give you the confidence to do anything. You only need to know how to manage it well and what to do. Read on to find out how to do it!

Why Good Mental Health Is So Important For Young Adults

As soon as you become 18 years old, you are known as an adult. However, the logical part of a teenager's brain keeps growing until around 25 years old. It means that young adults still rely on the emotional aspect of their brains as they develop. The decisions of young adults start to make more sense when you know this.

Already this might have given you an "A-ha!" moment. Your unusual, random decisions might surprise you, your parents, and other adults. But, as explained above, it is out of your control. **It is all part and parcel of the journey of adulting.** Psychologists refer to it as "extended adolescence."

As your brain matures through this period, it will feel like a transition for you. Similar to when you went through puberty. The changes you experience in your brain, hormones, and life experiences can affect you emotionally. These effects, in turn, can also affect your mental health.

According to a study by the University of California San Francisco (UCSF), 48% of young adults struggled with mental health in the middle of 2021. Sadly, many people overlook the mental health struggles of young adults. Additionally, there are certain situations where young adults are at more risk of developing mental health problems.

Here are some examples:

- **Abuse By Parents**
  Physical or psychological abuse from parents can affect children in many ways. Children can have unfulfilling relationship patterns, a lack of compassion, strained coping skills, and severe mental illness later in life.

- **Nutrition**
  Poor nutrition can take its toll on young adults. In adulthood, it can affect your academic achievement and emotional struggles. Food insecurity can cause malnutrition and stress, which can increase anxiety.

- **Drug Abuse**
  Young adults that suffer from anxiety or depression can sometimes get involved in substance abuse. It's a form of self-medicating to feel better. However, it makes people worse, and mental health problems go undetected.

How To Deal With Your Mental Well-being

Good mental health and wellness can help you grow positively and lead a successful life. Identifying coping mechanisms for dealing with mental illness can be life-changing if you experience issues. Here are three areas that can help you:

Learning To Build Resilience

Building your resilience can help counter anxiety and depression. If you have built resilience, you can handle new stress, significant traumatic events, or losses. There are many ways in which you can build this resilience:

- Go out and make friends/social connections and meet up regularly.
- Get involved in organizations that help others.
- Realize that changes are inevitable as you grow.
- Break up goals. You'll feel less stressed (more about this in the next chapter).

Identifying When You Have Unhealthy Thoughts

If you recognize that you have a lot of unhealthy thoughts, don't ignore them. Share your concerns with somebody close to you. Discussing your mental health is not a taboo subject. It "gets it out there," so you can have an open and honest discussion.

Seeking Out Mental Health Counselling

Take it a step further and seek professional help. **It is the most positive thing you can do.** You have recognized that you might have a mental health issue. A counselor can help you manage it now so that you can take control of your life.

The Magical Link Between Physical and Mental Health

If you always thought physical and mental health were separate, you must think again. The two areas are so connected it is impossible to separate them. When one is good, it can help to improve the other and vice versa.

Learning how they work together can help you manage them as best as possible.

Signs That Your Mental Health Is Declining

Studies have shown that when you are in an excellent mental state, you can also stay physically healthy. For example, a positive outlook on life can reduce your heart attack or stroke risk. **Being happy can also reduce inflammation in the body.**

On the flip side, if your mental health declines, your physical health can also. For example, research shows a link between depression and health problems like cancer, chronic pain, thyroid problems, and multiple sclerosis.

Signs That Your Physical Health Is Declining

It's easy to get complacent and take your physical health for granted. However, when your physical health declines, it can be a shock. For example, you can feel powerless if you break your leg, are in pain, and have restricted movement.

This situation also applies if you develop a more serious illness, like a chronic disease, cancer, heart attack, or stroke, it's hard to stay optimistic, and you can become depressed. This depression can then affect your mental health.

5 Mental Health Tips To Help You

You're at a new stage in your life where you want to be more independent. You want to create and live a lifestyle that matches your ideals and beliefs. With all this comes intense feelings and emotions as you move through adulthood.

Here are some pointers to consider when it comes to mental health. It helps you deal with a situation better or at least put steps in place to do so. Use these tips to protect yourself and your mental health.

1. Mental Health Conditions Have Multiple Causes

According to mental health research, 30% to 40% of mental health disorders are because of genetic causes. Also, 60% to 70% are because of a child's environment from childhood onwards.

Consequently, mental health conditions don't happen because of character faults or physical characteristics. It's because of chemical imbalances in the brain or stress and trauma from childhood experiences.

2. All Emotions Are Not Bad

A human needs to experience all the different emotions. Most negative emotions have the label of being "bad." People generally suppress emotions perceived as bad, such as being anxious, angry, fearful, or sad.

It would be best to express your feelings and emotions rather than suppress them. Because if you hide your emotions, it might feel better at the time, but it could lead to negative consequences in your future life.

3. Monitor The Effect Of New Changes

When you are a teenager or young adult, you will experience many ups and downs. It is normal to feel affected when changes happen. Intense feelings can affect what you want or need daily.

If you feel that any new or sudden change makes you feel drastically different, it's best to seek help.

It's better to take action to help yourself. Otherwise, things could get worse for you. Don't be afraid to admit when something is wrong, and you feel different. Getting the help you need is the best way to handle feelings like this.

4. Understand That Social Media Can Affect Anybody

Social media can affect anybody at any stage of their lives. It can have many negative effects. For example, by comparing your life to others, you can start obsessing about what you should and shouldn't be doing.

You can become so caught up in social media that it can affect how you act "in the real world." You must use social media healthily and balance the time you spend on it. Too much social media can start to take over your life.

5. There Is No Connection Between Your Self-Worth And Outcomes

You might feel pressured to perform well academically or feel imposter syndrome in your work. Many young people compare themselves to their peers to see how well they perform.

It's imperative to remember that your self-worth is not limited to your achievements in life. **Most importantly, it would help if you felt positive about yourself, regardless of what you do in your life.**

These Things Do Not Define Your Self-Worth

It's easy to get caught up in your self-worth and worry about where you are. You can let these connections go and feel happy for who you are. Yes, wanting to progress in life and develop yourself is excellent. But everything will come at the right time in your life. You don't need to push it or tie it to something else in your life.

Your Current Job

You might have a job you love or a job you hate, or perhaps you don't even have a job. It is important to remember that your job situation doesn't matter. People should respect you with dignity and respect whatever you do.

The Amount Of Money You Have In The Bank

You may be living from paycheck to paycheck. If you are, it doesn't mean you are any less than somebody with loads of money in the bank. **Money does not make a person.** Your value is in being you.

Your Physical Appearance

The "halo effect" can make people think that somebody who is attractive or gives a good impression is a fantastic person. Don't think you must look a certain way to be perceived well. **Be your original self and own it!**

Your Current To-Do List

Feeling like a failure if you don't complete a to-do list is not productive. **It is destructive.** Being a successful person can take some time. Having a to-do list is not everything. Stick to your plan, and you will get there.

Your Age

Many young adults feel they need more life experiences. Or that people will not take them seriously. Forget all thoughts like this. **Your age is entirely irrelevant. Just google 'young famous entrepreneurs' and you'll know what I mean.**

Your Social Media Following

Ten followers, or one thousand followers on social media, is irrelevant. **Putting your comments out there and expecting interactions is a recipe for disaster.** Write something if you want, and let those who wish to interact do so.

Your Qualifications

If you didn't manage to get your college degree, so what! It doesn't make you less intelligent than somebody who did get one. Never let anybody look down on you because you didn't get a qualification.

Your Current Relationship Status

Many young people find being single challenging, as they feel unseen pressure to be in a relationship. **View it differently and think about your happiness.** Learn to love being by yourself and enjoying who you are.

The Number Of Friends You Have

The amount of friends you have doesn't mean anything. You might only want a few friends because that is what you like. If somebody thinks it's strange you only have a few friends, that is their issue, not yours.

What Other People Think Of You

Some people get involved and worry about what other people think about them. **It's your life, and you are in control.** You are a valuable person, and you don't need anybody else, whoever they are, to tell you your self-worth.

Use These 5 Steps To Protect Your Mental Health

You can follow five easy steps to ensure you are looking after your mental health. Check them out below.

1. **Always Ask For Help When You Need It**
   If you need help, ask for it. You can't rely on somebody else to notice that you need help. You might have put up a big front, and everybody thinks you are fine. **Don't be scared to reach out to somebody.**

2. **Recognize The Signs**
   Be honest with yourself and recognize the signs. If you start acting differently or don't feel comfortable with yourself, it could be a sign that something is wrong. Take notice.

3. **Talk About The Issue With Somebody Else**
   Talking with somebody about one of your concerns can help immensely. The old saying can apply, "A problem shared is a problem halved." Speak to somebody and let them give you their take on your problem.

4. **Remember Not To Stay Inside Your Head**
   Whatever you do, remember not to stay in your head. Overthinking can make you feel crazy. You won't know if you are coming or going, and it can make it difficult for you to make the right decisions in life.

5. **Look After Your Physical Health**
   As mentioned earlier in this chapter, remember the intricate connection between your physical and mental health. Try and make an effort to do something physical every day, even if it is a short walk. **It will keep your spirits up!**

Eating Well Can Help Your Physical and Mental Health

Eating the right things is another easy way to help your physical and mental health. Read on to find out the best foods. **You might be surprised what an avocado or sweet potato can do for you!**

18 Foods To Boost Your Physical And Mental Health

Type of Food	Main Benefits
Avocadoes	<ul><li>A source of unsaturated fat that can help your brain cells.</li><li>It can aid in reducing blood pressure.</li><li>It can decrease the risk of cognitive decline.</li></ul>
Beans	<ul><li>Chickpeas and lentils have fiber and antioxidants.</li><li>It can help with blood sugar levels.</li><li>It contains thiamine which is good for memory.</li></ul>
Berries	<ul><li>It can repair cells and combat inflammation.</li><li>Improve symptoms of anxiety and depression.</li><li>Increase your attention span and concentration.</li></ul>
Broccoli	<ul><li>It contains vitamins A, C, and K and can fight cancer.</li><li>It can combat anxiety, fatigue, and depression.</li></ul>
Dark Chocolate	<ul><li>Stimulants for focus and concentration.</li><li>It has flavanols that are anti-inflammatory.</li><li>It can help to improve your mood.</li></ul>
Eggs	<ul><li>Egg yolks can keep the eyes healthy.</li><li>It can protect your skin from UV damage.</li><li>It can help with brain development.</li></ul>
Leafy Greens	<ul><li>Excellent for mental health. Eating collard greens, for example, can improve cognitive functions.</li></ul>
Nuts and Seeds	<ul><li>Walnuts have Omega-3 acids - which are good for heart health and can improve cholesterol.</li><li>Seeds can reduce the risk of cancer and diabetes.</li></ul>

Oily Fish	• Omega-3 fatty acid helps with memory and brain health. • Boost positive mental health and lower anxiety.
Oranges	• Contain a high level of Vitamin C. • It helps to produce white blood cells and antibodies.
Quinoa	• This grain is full of fiber, iron, and proteins. • It helps with weight and can reduce heart disease risk.
Spinach and Kale	• Spinach can create healthy new cells. • Kale reduces the risk of breast and ovarian cancer.
Sweet Potato	• It helps to strengthen the immune system. • Vitamin A helps with bone and eye health.
Tea	• It helps to prevent Alzheimer's, cancer, and diabetes. • It can promote healthier bones, gums, and teeth. • It can enhance focus, memory, and mood.
Tomatoes	• It contains lycopene which can prevent cancer. • It protects the skin from UV rays. • Decreases cholesterol levels.
Unprocessed Food	• Always try to eat unprocessed food. Because processed food can lead to hyperactivity or depression.
Wholegrains	• Contain tryptophan, which helps make serotonin, the "good" hormone, which can improve your mood and help you sleep better.
Yogurt	• It has probiotics which can help digestion. • It can influence a person's physical and mental well-being by decreasing anxiety, depression, and stress.

How Exercise Can Boost Your Mental Health

Staying active is a great way to boost your mental health. There are exercises for everybody. It doesn't matter what fitness level you are. Read on to find out the best physical activities for mental health.

There are four types of exercise: balance, cardiovascular, flexibility, and strength training. Studies have found that all kinds of exercise can help with mental health. Also, people who did team sports had fewer bad mental health days.

If team exercises aren't your thing, research has shown that these four individual exercises are also great for your mental health:

- **Aerobics or gym exercises**
  These types of exercises can help to promote good mental health. Some examples would be boxing, rope skipping, rowing, or weightlifting.

- **Cycling**
  Cycling has multiple mental health benefits. It can reduce anxiety, depression, and stress. It can also help to improve your self-esteem, get into mindfulness practice, and helps you to socialize.

- **Running**
  Running has been seen to help people with ADHD. It can help people who have ADHD control their thoughts, slow down, and have more focus.

- **Yoga**
  It can help to reduce stress and relieve anxiety, depression, and insomnia. Reducing stress levels can help people who have uncontrollable negative thoughts.

These are all suggestions on exercises you can do to help your mental and physical health. However, doing any exercise you love can help your mental state and boost your positivity.

How Sleep Can Boost Your Physical and Mental Health

Sleeping is a potent tool that can help your physical and mental health. If you don't get enough sleep, it can affect your life in many ways. Here are a few examples:

- Minor problems can seem a lot worse than they are.
- It can affect your mood and outlook on life.
- It can affect your patience levels.

The best thing you can do to counter this is to create a sleeping schedule that works best for you. You can commit to getting enough sleep each night. Also, limit your screen time before bed so your brain is calmer and you can sleep more easily.

How To Take Care Of Your Mental Health

It is worth remembering that if you are struggling with mental health issues, it is best to see professional help. However, many different techniques can help promote positive mental health.

Here are some things you can do to improve your mental health.

Meditation And Mindfulness Can Hit The Right Spots

Two techniques that are linked together are the practices of mindfulness and meditation. The National Institute for Health and Care Excellence (NICE) recommends mindfulness to manage depression.

Research has also shown that meditation can help with depression, aggression, addiction, and anxiety. You don't need to know about meditation to do it. Start with a few minutes and work your way up.

(NB You will find some Mindfulness exercises in this chapter's "Interactive" section).

Make Sure Your Stay Connected With People

Maintaining relationships with family, friends, and neighbors can benefit the mental health of individuals. Also, social interaction, such as volunteering, can help to boost your health.

Staying in contact with people and not alienating yourself can keep your spirits up. If you find it challenging to meet people in person, you can always call them, have a video chat, or send a message.

Always Be Kind To Yourself

It's also important to look after yourself and don't put yourself under any pressure. Try to take some time out of your day, even if it is only 15-30 minutes. It can help you to de-stress and lift your mood.

You could also treat yourself to a nice meal, a luxurious bath, or a massage. Do something special for yourself. It could be anything as long as it gives you a timeout and makes you feel great.

Make An Effort To Learn Something New

Learning something new can help to boost your confidence and self-esteem. It can be a new skill that you learn, or you could take up a new hobby. It's a great way to have a sense of purpose and meet new people.

An Interactive Element to Reset Your Body and Mind

You have come to the next interactive element of the book. In this section, I will go through some easy mindfulness exercises that you can do yourself. It can help to balance yourself and give your body and mind the perfect reset.

Mindfulness Exercises

These mindfulness exercises are especially with young adults in mind. Mindfulness is all about making you aware of your thoughts and feelings. Try to work your way through them all and find one or two that you enjoy the most.

Write in a Journal

Spend some time each day writing in a journal. Don't plan what you will write. The best way is to sit down and let it flow. Journaling can help you to:

- Manage anxiety
- Cope with depression
- Reduce stress
- Help you prioritize the different things in your life

Set up Mantras

Mantras can help you "will" things into your life. It is usually a phrase that means something to you. You can say a mantra, make it part of a song, or chant it. Mantras help remind you that you can achieve anything if you put your mind to it.

You must vocalize a mantra and repeat it. You need to open your mind and feel what you are saying when you use the mantra. It will make the mantra more effective for you.

You can follow this process to meditate with a mantra:

- ★ Find a mantra you like or create a new one
- ★ Think about your intentions and why the words are important to you
- ★ Go to a comfortable place, sit down, cross your legs and relax
- ★ Concentrate on your breathing as you inhale and exhale
- ★ Say your mantra out loud several times
- ★ Notice how it feels on your lips and goes around your body

Top Tip

You can come up with new mantras for different situations in your life.

Do A Body Scan

A body scan can help you become more familiar with your body. You can slow everything down and become more aware of how your body feels in different areas. It is a great way to center yourself and gain more focus.

You can do a body scan by:

- ★ Finding a place that is quiet and where you can be alone.
- ★ It has to be somewhere you can stay for 15 to 20 minutes without interruption.
- ★ Get into a comfortable position, as you will stay in the same pose.
- ★ Take a deep breath, then focus on an area of your body.
- ★ Think about that area of the body and use all your senses.
- ★ Once you have finished that area, move on to another body part.
- ★ The end of the exercise is when you have done your whole body.

The body scan can help you gain a better understanding of your body. You can find where the aches and pains are, and it can help you to slow down.

Write a List of Gratitude

A gratitude list is a great thing to do at the end of the day. It can finish your day perfectly, especially if you have had a challenging day. It can help to ground you and get rid of any stress.

You can make your gratitude list by:

- ★ Grabbing a pen and some paper or using your mobile phone to make a list.
- ★ Make a list of things that happened during the day that made you feel grateful.
- ★ Once you have written down five things you have finished the task.

Top Tip

Don't let things upset you in your day. You are in control of your happiness, not anybody else. **If someone upsets you it means they have control over you.**

Do Some Breathing Exercises

Breathing exercises help center you and keep you in the moment. For example, if you have an exam, a prom, or any other big event. A few minutes of deep breathing can help to make you feel better.

There are many breathing exercises, but the easiest one is diaphragmatic breathing. When you use this type of breathing, you are engaging your diaphragm muscle, at the bottom of your lungs.

You can do this type of breathing by:

- ★ Sit straight or lie down on your back, whatever you prefer. Bend your knees so your feet are flat on the floor.
- ★ Put one hand on your chest and the other hand just below your belly button on your stomach.
- ★ Breathe in through your nose slowly. Let your stomach expand as your lungs fill with air. Your stomach will also rise as you inhale.
- ★ Now you need to exhale through your mouth. Let your stomach go down as the air goes out of the lungs.
- ★ You can do this several times until you feel calmer.

Top Tip

You can do this exercise anywhere! If you are about to take an exam, you are in the middle of an argument with somebody, or you are having a lunch break. It will immediately make you feel calmer and more in control.

Go For A Mindful Walk

This exercise can help you focus on the present moment, and you can get some exercise. You only need to have a place to walk and some comfortable shoes. You can do it alone or with someone else.

You can do a mindful walk by:

- ★ Pick a walk where you are less likely to be stopped by anybody for a chat.
- ★ Focus on your surroundings not where you are going.
- ★ As you are walking, pay attention to your body.
- ★ Think about your feet and legs and what they are doing.
- ★ Listen to your breathing as you walk.

- ★ Pay attention to your surroundings and notice the sights, sounds, and smells.
- ★ If your mind wanders somewhere, bring it back to the now.
- ★ When you have finished the walk, reflect on your experience.

Mindful walking can turn a regular walk into something special. It will help you feel relaxed and rejuvenated, ready to take on the rest of the day ahead!

Chapter Four Summary

In this chapter, the focus was on your wellness. You learned about the connection between your physical and mental health. We looked at the type of food you can eat and the exercises you can do to help your health. You also have some mindfulness exercises to help you stay balanced and calm.

In the next chapter, you will learn about money skills and ways to achieve financial independence. Living alone can be costly, but you can learn how to manage your money. By the end of the chapter, you will feel more confident with your money and how to use it correctly.

REVIEW PAGE

CREATING THE LIFE, YOU ALWAYS WANTED TO HAVE

"When you're young, everything feels like the end of the world, but it's not; it's just the beginning."

—**ZAC EFRON**

You might have made some mistakes already in your life. But it's never too late to create the life you always wanted. You only need to follow the right steps.

At the beginning of the book, I took you back to the basics, so you can learn everything you need to be independent at a young age. You learned important kitchen skills you can use for the rest of your life. Also, create a meal for your family and friends to showcase your new independence.

This firm education led to essential skills to handle home emergencies and repair and maintenance skills to help save you money. You no longer need to call your parents or anybody else for help. Because you now have more confidence to handle situations and make the right decisions.

You've also read one of the most important chapters and understand the importance of your physical and mental health. Finding balance in your life will be key to everything working well. Remember to use the mindfulness exercises in that chapter to look after your well-being.

By leaving a review of this book on Amazon, you'll show other young adults where to find guidance to improve their life skills.

I appreciate your support. It will encourage people to buy the book and try new things, so they can improve their lives, just like you are right now.

You still have some reading and learning but are on a clear path to success. Keep reading the book to discover how you can achieve financial freedom, and improve your personal and professional relationships and career. You will also learn how to set the right goals to lead you to a happy and successful life!

ID
THE MONEY GAME: ACHIEVE FINANCIAL INDEPENDANCE

"Wealth is largely the result of habit."
—JOHN JACOB ASTOR

Money makes the world go round, and it pays the bills. But it's not easy earning it and saving it when the cost of living is so high. Money could be tight if you still depend on your parents for financial support or have just started your career. However, being financially independent is possible with some planning and know-how.

Gain financial independence and enjoy freedom.

When you have a better understanding of how money works, you can take control of your financial situation and make it better. You don't need a math degree or become tight with your money. You only need to learn the right money skills to make your money work better.

Show me the money!

In this chapter, you will learn why it is so important to be money savvy at a young age. You will also find tips on budgeting, saving, and how to pay off debt. You'll also learn how to grow your money through different investments. These money management skills will help you have more money so you can do what you want to in your life.

Why Financial Education Is Important At A Young Age

Financial education is an essential life skill everyone should try to learn at a young age. **It can positively boost your well-being and open opportunities in your life.** If you are already managing your money well, move on to the next chapter. If you want to learn more about money and how to use it well, then you're in for a treat so please do read on.

When you understand how money works, you can start earning and investing from a young age. It can help you avoid lifelong money struggles. Sadly, schools do not educate young children on how to manage money. However, it is a critical life skill that can affect you throughout your life.

Smart Saving Tips You Can Use Right Now

Thinking about saving money can be a little daunting if you haven't done it before. You might think you only have enough money to get by every month. However, there are always ways to start saving, even if you don't have much.

Here are some tips so you can start saving some money:

Open Your First Savings Account

One of the easiest ways to start saving is to open a savings account. Look for a high-interest-rate savings account with a bank. In most cases, you don't need a lot of money upfront. Have a look online and shop around to find the best savings account with the highest interest rate.

Start A Budget

A budget can help you organize your money so you are not randomly spending it here and there. First, make a list of your income and all your expenses. **This exercise will help you see where you spend your money.** Once you have a realistic idea of how much money you can use each month, stick to it.

Reduce Your Expenses

It's not only about budgeting! It would help if you reduced your spending habits. An easy way to do this is to look at all your expenses. **You will then have a clear picture of what you buy and can reduce it.** You can also buy cheaper brands of clothes and food. Also, think about changing your energy supplier.

Get The Piggy Bank Out

In our technological society, it is easy to go straight to an app to help you budget or save. Alternatively, you can go old school and use a piggy bank or coin jar. You won't have to pay any fees, and you can visually see your money increase. It's a convenient way to save loose change that can add up to a considerable amount quickly.

Eliminate Your Debt

To save properly, you must get rid of your debt. Clearing your debt depends on what type of debt you have. You could clear any debt with a high-interest rate or get rid of the smallest debt first. Once you are debt-free, you can concentrate more on saving.

Effective Budgeting Strategies

Now you know a little more about how to get a handle on your finances. It's good to look in more detail at different types of budgeting strategies. There is a lot of advice out there, but you need to use techniques that will be effective for you. Budgeting can help you have a clear action plan of what to do with your money.

Know Your Income Inside Out

The most important thing to know before you start budgeting is the proper amount of your income. **This figure is also known as "take-home" pay.** It is the amount you have each month after you have taken the tax off your paycheck.

You might have income from different sources on top of your paycheck. For example, you might have a side hustle and get government assistance or child support. Whatever it is, remove any tax amounts and add all the different incomes together.

This figure will be your total income after taxes.

Top Tip

If you are self-employed, your income will fluctuate. Therefore, it is best to look at your lowest income earning month and base your budget on that.

Choose The Best Budgeting Strategy For You

Budgeting can feel overwhelming, especially if this is your first time doing it. But don't worry. By the end of this chapter, you will feel far more confident about managing your money. Here are some different budgeting strategies to pick the best one for you!

50/30/20 Budgeting

One of the most simple budgeting strategies is 50/30/20. You'll need to split your income into three different categories. These categories are: needs, wants, and savings. Here is a little table to help illustrate it for you:

Your Take-Home Pay	Budget Category	Type Of Expenses
50%	Needs	Food, rent/mortgage, transportation, utilities
30%	Wants	Eating out, entertainment, shopping, vacations
20%	Savings	Debt payoff, emergency fund, retirement

Zero-based Budgeting

When you want complete control of every dollar you earn and spend, zero-based budgeting is for you! You allocate money towards your expenses and then to your goals in a clear manner.

For example, you allocate the money you need for your expenses. Then, with the money you have left, you will decide where to use it. It could be a goal to pay off debt or to put it in a savings account. You can redo your budget for this system every month.

Cash Envelope

This method is very hands-on. If you know you are a big spender, this system could be a total match for you. You will need to label some envelopes for every category in your budget, e.g., groceries, transportation, etc.

You will put the actual cash into each envelope. Once the money has gone, you cannot spend anything on that item for the rest of the month. Sounds brutal? It is, but it is very effective in helping you control your money.

Always Give Yourself A Margin

Tracking your money all the time can feel boring for some people after a while. Therefore, you can give yourself a margin to jump over this hurdle and not worry about it. Giving yourself a margin of error each month helps to provide you with some breathing room in your budget.

Creating A Margin

You can create a margin by identifying how much of your income you don't need to spend each month. **This amount is known as your buffer or your margin.** Your margin can be affected by things that happen in life. But try your best to stick to it each month.

Remember To Pay Yourself First

Finding money to save can be challenging if you have a lot of expenses. You can get around this by budgeting for your savings first. Then you can pay your bills with what you have left. This system is a "Paying yourself first" method. You can set up an automated payment to a savings account to help you.

You Can Use A Budgeting App To Help You

The methods above are all easy to use. But if you like to use apps, a budgeting app can help you take your budgeting to the next level. An app can give you instant access to your budget. You can see all your income and expenses in a few buttons. It's convenient if you need to make some quick purchase decisions.

Keep Track Of Your Progress

Budgeting is a spending plan. You will see what is and isn't working for you by tracking your progress. This information will help you change your spending habits. You might also want to change your budgeting system until you find one that works.

Budgeting Mistakes People Make

Nobody is perfect, and it is easy to make mistakes in life. If you mess up, don't worry about it. You can get back on track the following month. Here are some common mistakes people make, so you can keep them in mind when you are budgeting. Make sure you follow these guidelines to stop you from making the same mistakes:

- Put a margin of error in place
- Don't be too restrictive
- Track your spending habits
- Put some money aside for an emergency fund
- Review your budget system regularly

How To Pay Off Debt In Less Than A Year

You might have debt that you want to clear. Try out these strategies below to help you eliminate it in a year or at least remove a big chunk of it.

Raise Your Debt Repayment Percentage

You can put 15% of your income towards credit card debt and other loans. Usually, you only have to pay 2% of the outstanding balance each month to credit card companies. Paying more can help you to pay your debts off a lot quicker.

Use Some Of Your Savings To Pay Off Expensive Debts

It's great to save, but you can use some of your savings to pay off high-interest debts. It might feel strange to use it to pay off debt. However, many savings accounts have low-interest rates, so it makes more sense to pay off high-interest loans.

Ask For A Lower Interest Rate

You don't get anything unless you ask! Speak to your creditors and negotiate a lower interest rate. You might be pleasantly surprised by how easy this is. If you pay your bills regularly and have money in your account, they won't object.

Make Use Of Tax Refunds

A tax refund is always exciting and as soon as you see it you are already spending it in your mind. Change your way of thinking, and use it to pay off your debt. You didn't have the money anyway, so you might as well use it for something more impactful.

Sell Things You Don't Need

Have a good look around your home and see if you can sell anything. You might have some things you could sell on eBay or Craigslist. Or arrange a garage sale and sell everything you don't need. Use your earnings to pay off some more debt.

Review Your Life Insurance

You can cash in your life insurance and pay a chunk off your debt. It makes sense to do this if you don't have a partner or children. NB, It only works for whole-life policies with cash value, not for a term life insurance policy.

Vow To Earn More Money

If you want to pay off your debt in less than a year, you can decide to earn more money. You can take on a part-time job or negotiating a higher wage from you manager.

Consider A Credit Card Balance Transfer

You might ignore these offers when you get them in the post. But it could be worth considering if you want to pay your debt off fast. Move all your high-rate debt to a 0% interest-rate deal. If it lasts for 12 months, you can eliminate all credit card interest.

Eliminate Old Debt With The Statute Of Limitations

You could focus on paying current debt and forgoing payment on bills 7 or 10 years older. Each state has its own rules about debt, so you should look into it. But if the statute of limitations has passed, you can forgo payment.

Get Rid Of Credit Card Debts By Filing For Bankruptcy

Only do this is you are completely stuck and need help paying off your debt. However, this is a good option if you have no income and high credit card and medical bills. A Chapter 7 bankruptcy filing can clear all your credit card debts.

Why You Should Invest At An Early Age

Investing might seem like a scary thing to do if you don't know anything about it. But it is worth investing when you are as young as possible. Your older self will thank you for it, as you will be more financially stable as you get older.

Here are some benefits of investing earlier in life:

- **Take Advantage of Compounding Interest**
  By investing when you are younger, you take advantage of compound interest. Compounding is a process of earning returns on investments and then reinvesting to make more returns.

- **Reaching Financial Goals Quickly**
  If you invest when you are younger, you can reach your financial goals quickly. When you are older, you have to save money each month to invest. Doing it when you are young, means you will spend less to reach your goals.

- **Get Into Good Financial Habits**
  Investing when you are a young adult gets you into good financial habits. You will be used to putting money aside each month. It's a great mindset and will put you in a strong financial position when you are older.

Wise Investment Ideas For Young Adults

Investing involves placing money into financial products and hoping for a return. You are not guaranteed to make a profit, so you must do your research. Here are some investment ideas for young adults, to give you a fantastic financial start.

Bank Deposits

You could make bank deposits every month. Saving money in this way is a form of investing. If you deposit money into a bank account regularly, the money will add up over time. It's a low-risk investment, especially if your bank is secure. You will always know how much money is in the account.

Mutual Funds

This type of investment is different from a bank deposit. Investment funds are collective investments. The investment can consist of many investors.

You give your money to a management company. This company invests in various financial products. The income from these investments goes to all individual investors.

Real Estate

Investing in real estate is a solid investment. The two main property investment methods are value appreciation and rental income.

You can buy a property, and the value can increase; this is value appreciation. You can then sell the property and make money. Alternatively, you can rent the property and receive a monthly income from your tenant.

Life Insurance

This insurance is a contract between the insurance policyholder and an insurer. The insurer pays money to a designated beneficiary when the insured person dies.

There are many ways you can make money from life insurance. You can sell it as an investment, or you can use it as funds for when you retire. You can also use it to pay for final expenses and estate taxes.

Stock Market

Stock investing is another great way to build long-term wealth. Companies issue stocks to raise money. Investors buy stock shares to get a return on investment.

You need to decide how much you will invest in stocks and open an investment account. Do your research to determine which stocks you want to invest in, and then continue reinvesting as you make money.

Unit-Linked Insurance Plans

A Unit-Linked Insurance Plan can reward investors with significant returns. It combines the protection of life insurance with the potential for investment gains.

A portion of your payment goes to life insurance. The rest goes into a pool of money consisting of shares, debt, or a mixture of both. You receive units from your investment in the pool. The value of these units can go up and down..

Other Short-Term Investments

There are also other types of short-term investments that you can look into. These types of investments are safe and also provide liquidity. You only need to invest what you can afford at the time. Examples of such investments are emergency funds, money market funds, savings accounts, and short-term cash deposits.

Everything Is Possible When It Comes To Money

I have hands-on experience with the highs and lows of dealing with money. At the tender age of 17, I worked in a bank and learned a lot about money and finance in general - bank accounts, mortgages, credit cards, finance agreements, loans, etc.

This education in money was great, but I was too young to understand how devastating debt can be and how it can all spiral so quickly. I knew all the ins and outs of money but ended up racking over $20,000 in debt. It was a challenging period in my life to say the least.

I then took steps in my twenties and cleared all my debt and loans. I was even working 3 jobs over 7 days a week for a year. This experience taught me a hard lesson, and it is one I am grateful for. Rest assured it can be solved if you are in this predicament by following the simple guidelines below:

- ★ Calculate how much you earn - this can be weekly or monthly or whatever works for you.
- ★ Workout your Expenses.
- ★ Use your disposable income to pay off your debtors and work out how long this will take.
- ★ If you are struggling to keep up with the minimum payments I would recommend contacting all your creditors to explain your situation and request they freeze any interest or charges, so whatever you pay back will come off the debt.
- ★ If you feel the debts are going to take longer than expected to be paid, then I would look at ways you can earn additional income.
- ★ Stay committed and disciplined in your approach and you will get to the finish line.

Summary

You now know why investing early in life is a good idea. It can help to make your life more financially stable, and you can reach your financial goals more quickly. You also have several methods to budget your money to make it last longer. All these financial skills will help you later in life.

The next chapter will examine interpersonal skills and how you can improve your relationships. It will explain why they are essential, and you can learn strategies to help you improve them. You'll also learn about different communication skills and how they can help you be more assertive.

06

POSITIVE CONNECTIONS: DEVELOPING INTERPERSONAL SKILLS FOR EVERYDAY LIFE

"Seek first to understand, then to be understood."
—**STEPHEN COVEY**

Everybody wants to get on with everybody else, but it's not always easy. Relationships can be challenging, and sometimes it can be hard to bond with people. We all have different personalities, and relationships with your family will differ from those with your friends and colleagues.

Happy relationships can enrich your life.

Improving your interpersonal skills needs to be high on your list of priorities. You might think you are connecting with people correctly, but there are always things you can do better. It's important to remember that everybody is an individual, and there are good and bad people in the world.

You can learn not to take things personally.

This chapter will explain the importance of having good interpersonal skills. It will also give you strategies on how to improve them. You'll gain the confidence to deal with difficult people and situations in all areas of your life. It can also help you to enhance your relationships with your parents, friends, and colleagues.

What Are Interpersonal Skills?

You use interpersonal skills when you communicate with other people. There are a variety of skills when it comes to interacting with people. But the most used ones are your communication and listening skills. Your interpersonal skills also cover your ability to control and manage your emotions when interacting with others.

You'll also find interpersonal skills are known as life skills, people skills, social skills, or soft skills. **How good are your interpersonal skills right now? Do they need some improvement?** Interpersonal skills are a huge part of being successful in life.

If you are a great communicator, it can help you in any work situation. You will also be able to mix easily in a group and make friends easily. You don't have to be an extrovert to mix with people. Some of the best communicators in the world are introverts like Bill Gates and Warren Buffet.

It's all about "giving off" a feeling of trust when you engage with people. It might not come naturally at first, but over time you can use your interpersonal skills to great effect. It can also help to strengthen your personal relationships. You feel more confident explaining how you feel and are open to listening to the needs of others.

Why You Need To Have Interpersonal Skills

It's all about developing an awareness of how you interact with different people. You might have to communicate with people at different levels. Interpersonal skills can help you with this. For example, most of us spend a great deal of time at work. It is, therefore, essential that you can build strong relationships with all your colleagues.

You also have to communicate with other students and teachers while studying at school or university. Or you might end up in a completely random situation with strangers. This situation can be daunting if you don't know how to deal with it.

Here are a few different ways in which interpersonal skills can help you in your life:

- You can treat others with empathy and respect.
- You start to understand different situations and how you need to act.
- You can improve relationships overall and build trust.
- Learn how to use patience and not get stressed over minor issues.
- It helps you demonstrate leadership skills and the confidence to lead people.

Interpersonal Skills Include The Following

You can break interpersonal skills down into many different types of skills that you can use. Here are the main areas so you know what is involved and what areas you need to improve.

Communication Skills

The ability to communicate effectively is one of the most important interpersonal skills. It enables us to pass the information on and understand what people say.

Verbal communication

This is how we use words to share information with people. Using the right words is essential so people can understand and interpret them correctly.

Non-verbal communication

This type of communication is without words. It is when we communicate with people with our body language. Your facial expressions, hand movements, and distance from speaking to somebody are all examples.

Listening skills

This refers to how we interpret non-verbal and verbal messages people send us. **You need to listen right to understand the actual message.** People can become frustrated or irritated if you don't listen well.

Emotional Intelligence

Managing the emotions of yourself and others, either individually or in a group. People with higher emotional intelligence can handle stress effectively and are less likely to suffer from depression.

Teamwork skills

You can work in groups and teams in formal and informal situations if you have teamwork skills. To work well in teams, you need to understand how they work and how familiarity can change group or team dynamics.

Negotiation, persuasion, and influencing skills

These interpersonal skills involve working with others to find Win/Win outcomes so everybody is happy. Without being able to negotiate with others, little conflicts can lead to arguments and feelings of resentment.

Conflict resolution and mediation

This type of communication involves working with others to resolve conflicts and disagreements positively. It's an excellent skill to have, as conflict can arise at work in stressful situations. Additionally, it can also happen in personal relationships.

Problem-solving and decision-making

It involves working with others to identify, define, solve problems, and decide the best course of action. These skills can also help you in work and personal situations.

How To Improve Your Communication Skills

Improving your communication skills can help you to interact with all kinds of people wherever you are. **Remember, it's not only about the words that you use.** There are different types of verbal and nonverbal cues that you use as well.

Verbal Communication

You can build rapport with people and have more positive, stronger relationships by improving your verbal communication skills. Here are some ways in which you can improve your verbal communication skills:

- **Take time to think before you speak**
  As a rule, people don't like silence in conversation. However, pausing before you answer a question can improve the quality of your responses.

  Likewise, if somebody you talk to pauses before they answer a question, don't interrupt them. It is polite and shows you are interested in what they say.

- **Keep Your Conversation Concise**
  Nobody wants to hear a long, rambling conversation. **It takes time and can become boring!** People understand things better when you are concise. It also gets your main messages across quickly. Also, try to use uncomplicated words when speaking or writing so everything is clear.

- **Put Yourself In Their Shoes**
  To communicate effectively, you need to understand your target audience. Explain things clearly, especially if it is complex or technical. Also, be respectful of different cultures or personalities. If you have to do a presentation, make sure it is specific to your audience.

- **Watch Your Tone**
  Using the right tone is crucial when using verbal communication. It can affect how people engage with you. **Try to use a friendly and warm tone with a smile.** Also, vary the level of your tone to keep people interested. You can also copy the other person's tone to increase engagement.

- **Use Active Listening**
  Give the other person your full attention when they are speaking. It shows interest and will understand their needs better. It helps to strengthen your relationship. If the person feels you are listening to them, they will do the same for you. **Try these out next time you speak with somebody:**

  ★ Focus on what the person is saying, not what you want to tell them.
  ★ Ask some clarifying questions to ensure you fully understand.
  ★ Don't make judgments or stereotype the person.
  ★ Always wait until the person finishes talking before you reply to them.

- **Speak Confidently**
  It would help if you sounded confident when you spoke. If you sound like you don't believe in what you are saying, your audience won't believe you as well. When you establish your authority and credibility, people will trust you. You can write some notes and practice before a planned conversation or presentation to help you.

- **Always Be Authentic**
  You can take inspiration from other communicators/speakers. But remember to be you. People will feel more drawn toward you if you are genuine and transparent. Also, don't be embarrassed if you don't know the answer to a question. Say you don't. **People will appreciate your honest approach.**

- **Practice Makes Perfect**
  You might think it is cliched, but it is true. Practice does make things perfect. **Practicing will help you develop your skills and gain confidence.** Remember to use your skills in real life as often as you can. You can also practice in front of a mirror and record your voice to check your progress.

- **Seek Honest Feedback**
  If you need to do a presentation, arrange some time to practice it in front of family or friends. Ask them to give your their honest feedback. You can ask them to point out what you did well and where to improve. Also, after you have done a presentation at work, you can ask your boss for feedback.

Non-verbal communication

Always remember how important non-verbal communication is. You might have a great experience talking with somebody. But the other person might not have felt the same way. In a face-to-face conversation, our non-verbal communication is sometimes the loudest. Here are some tips on how to keep your body language in check:

- **Keep Eye Contact**

    When you are talking to someone, you need to maintain eye contact. It shows them that your focus is on them and you are interested. **Remember not to avoid eye contact or to stare into somebody's eyes.** Both of these things can make the other person feel uncomfortable.

- **Use An Open Body Position**

    Standing in an open position is a friendly, positive stance. It is welcoming for the other person and puts them at ease. Always remember not to cross your arms in front of your body. It is a defensive posture, seen as a barrier. Try to keep your arms as relaxed as possible.

- **Sit Alongside And At An Angle**

    You are always looking for balance when you have a conversation with someone. If this is possible, sit alongside the other person at a slight angle rather than directly opposite. **It is more friendly and less aggressive.** Otherwise, the person might feel like you are interviewing them.

- **Stop Fidgeting**

    If you're a fidgeter, this is for you. You might fidget when you speak with people. It's important to know that it can feel very distracting for the other person. It can sometimes appear that you are bored, nervous, or uncomfortable. **Not a great way to make a first impression!**

Listening skills

When you use listening skills effectively. You are listening to the message given, not only the words used. Listen as much as you can to provide a thoughtful answer. To develop your listening skills, you can try doing some of the following tips to help you:

- ★ Give the speaker your complete attention and stay focused.
- ★ Use body language to show engagement, such as nodding and smiling.
- ★ Remember to use prompts, such as "Yes" and "uh huh."
- ★ Ask for specific examples if you need further clarification.
- ★ Don't interrupt or redirect the conversation.
- ★ Provide your opinions politely.

How To Improve Your Emotional Intelligence

Emotional intelligence is also known as emotional quotient or EQ. Remember, emotional intelligence is the ability to manage your emotions and use and understand them. You can use it positively to communicate effectively, defuse conflict, empathize with people, overcome challenges, and relieve stress.

There are four key attributes of emotional intelligence. These four areas are self-management, self-awareness, social awareness, and relationship management. Here are more details about each of these areas and how to improve these key skills:

- **Self-Management**
  If you want to use your EQ, you need to use your emotions to make informed decisions about your behavior. For example, you can lose control of your emotions and make bad decisions when stressed.

Try this:
Next time you feel stressed or have another strong emotion, **stay emotionally present.** Learn to receive upsetting information and not let it take over your thoughts or self-control. You can make the right choices, manage your emotions, take the initiative, and adapt.

- **Self-Awareness**

  Science has discovered that your current emotional experience usually reflects your early life experience. It can affect your ability to handle core feelings, such as anger, fear, joy, and sadness. If you had good emotional support as a child, you could use these emotions well in adult life.

  On the contrary, if you have terrible experiences, you will distance yourself from your emotions. Connecting with your feelings can help you understand how emotions influence your thoughts and actions. You can improve your EQ by reconnecting with core emotions and accepting them.

  Try this:
  The best way to become more self-aware is to practice mindfulness. **You can find some mindfulness exercises in the interactive element of Chapter Four.**

- **Social Awareness**

  This lets you recognize mainly nonverbal cues that people are communicating to you. Recognizing these cues is great, as it lets you know how people feel. You can understand how their emotions change and what is important to them.

  To be socially aware, you need to be more present. It's common for people to multitask, especially in a work environment. But sometimes, when you do this, you can miss important emotional shifts in other people. Disregarding this information can lead to misunderstanding the person.

Try this:

You can improve your social awareness by putting thoughts aside and focusing 100% on the interaction with the person. Follow the flow of the person's emotional responses, but be aware of your emotional changes. By paying attention to the reactions of others, you gain insight into your own.

- **Relationship Management**

    Once you are emotionally aware, you can start recognizing what other people are experiencing and feeling. You can then add to this and develop different emotional/social skills. These skills will help you improve your relationships, making them more effective and fulfilling.

    Try this:

    Pay attention to how you use non-verbal communication. It can help you to improve your relationships when you know what signs you "give off." Use humor and laughing to destress and balance yourself. Look upon conflicts as opportunities to resolve and strengthen your relationships.

How To Develop Your Teamwork Skills

Most employers like to employ people who are comfortable working in a team environment. Whether you prefer to work independently or in a team, learning to work in a group will always benefit your career and educational goals. You can develop your teamwork skills by following these seven tips:

1. Try Not To Complain

   Nobody likes complaints. The main reason why is that complaining doesn't achieve anything. Aim to be the person that can help to resolve the problem. **Stay positive and lift the people around you in the team.** It can eliminate the complainers and for you to be an example to them and those around you.

2. Don't Fight Over Who Gets The Credit

   It doesn't matter who did something well in the team to get the win. A win is a win for everyone. Fighting with something to take credit will alienate you from the rest of the group. There is no competition inside a team. You all need to work together and share the credit.

3. Communicate Continuously

   Communication is critical for all relationships, business and personal. The best teams share ideas and are honest with each other. That also applies to the good and bad stuff. Have regular brainstorming sessions to get ideas. Also, don't forget to have fun and do things outside of work with the team.

4. Set Some Ground Rules

   Creating ground rules for the team helps speed up meetings. For example, nobody should look at electrical devices during meetings so that everybody can pay attention.

5. Share Your Enthusiasm

   Don't feel embarrassed if you have a fantastic idea and want to share it with the team. **Your idea could be the next big thing since sliced bread!** Plus, your team members might share your passion and get excited if your idea is fantastic.

6. Be Transparent

   Don't become a keyboard warrior, write aggressive emails to team members, and then don't say anything to their faces. It's best to be upfront to resolve issues. Communicate professionally at all times. It will help to keep the relationships and the team strong.

7. Celebrate The Team's Wins

   When your team achieves something, make sure that the group celebrates it. It's easy to move on to the next project. But celebrating your successes can give you all a sense of accomplishment. It will also encourage the team to replicate the win in the future.

How To Improve Your Negotiation, Persuasion, and Influencing Skills

Your negotiation skills help you to discuss and reach mutually beneficial outcomes. Your powers of persuasion can convince others to take appropriate action. Your influencing skills are a combination of negotiation and persuasion skills.

Here are a few tips to improve your negotiation and persuasion skills:

Negotiation Skills

- ★ Listen to the arguments from the other side and assess their logic.
- ★ Clarify areas by asking questions about who, what, where, why, and when.
- ★ Identify the key issues.
- ★ Identify any areas where there is common ground.
- ★ Realize that there might be "outside influences" that are affecting the problem.
- ★ Always stay calm and be assertive, not aggressive.
- ★ Remember that "No!" is a powerful word that you can use.

Persuasion Skills

- ★ Always focus on the needs of the other person. You can gain trust and respect.
- ★ Do your research and put forward your case with clear logic.
- ★ Do not use hesitant language, such as "you know," "I mean," or "Ummm."
- ★ Use positive speech instead of negative language.
- ★ Compliment the other party about their efforts so that they warm to you.
- ★ Remember people's names, so you can treat them as an individual.

How To Develop Your Conflict Resolution And Mediation Skills

Conflict resolution and mediation skills can help you to strengthen and grow your personal and professional relationships. Here are some ways you can develop both sets of skills.

Conflict resolution

It's worth noting that conflict is not a bad thing. It can signify a healthy relationship as it is impossible for people to agree on everything all the time. Here are four different ways you can develop your conflict resolution skills:

1) **Relieve Stress As Quickly As You Can**
   You must try and stay calm and focused whenever there is a tense situation. You might feel overwhelmed if you don't know how to control yourself and stay centered. The best way to relieve stress is to use your senses. Use sights, sounds, touch, tastes, and smells that help to soothe you.

2) **Manage Your Emotions**

As discussed earlier in this chapter, emotional awareness is essential to understanding yourself and others. Aim to understand why you feel a certain way so that you can communicate effectively and solve problems. Don't be afraid to face your emotions to understand what is happening.

3) **Beef Up Your Nonverbal Communication Skills**
There is a lot of nonverbal communication flying around during conflicts and arguments. Watch the nonverbal communication of the other person. A calm tone or concerned facial expression can help diffuse a tense situation.

4) **Use Humor To Take The Sting Out Of The Tail**
You can avoid confrontations and resolve disagreements by communicating humorously or playfully. It can help you to express things less severely. However, make sure you laugh with the person and not at them! It can reduce tension and help put everything into perspective.

Mediation

When workplace conflict occurs, it can be challenging for some people to know what to do. You need somebody to step in, mediate and calm everything down. Because without control, it could escalate into an even bigger issue. Here are three things you can do to calm things down and act as a mediator.

1) **Immediately Create A Safe Environment**
Create an environment where both parties will feel safe, one where they can open up about their concerns and fears. Individuals need

to feel they can talk freely. This "psychologically-safe" place helps to build trust. It also allows both parties to express themselves fully.

2) **Make Sure The Parties Involved Feel Heard**

    People in conflict have a core desire to feel that people are listening to them. Listen like a mediator in silence to understand what is happening. Also, listen with an open mind without any judgment. It lets employees express themselves, process the situation, and devise solutions.

3) **Focus On Needs And Not Positions**

    A mediator needs to get people away from their fixed positions and mindsets. You must find out what is happening underneath and understand the real issues. Once you have this information, it is easier to deal with and resolve the situation.

How To Improve Your Problem-Solving And Decision-Making Skills

In life, you have to make crucial decisions every single day. Sometimes it can be hard to decide what to do. Plus, as you get older, these decisions can make more of an impact on your life. You can start making the right decisions by improving your problem-solving and decision-making skills.

Problem-solving

- First, you need to **identify** what the problem is. Once you know the problem, you can move on to the next stage.
- Now you need to **define** the main elements of the problem. You can break it down into small, manageable action steps that you need to take.
- At this point, you can now **examine** possible solutions to the problem. The trick is to look for easy, practical solutions. Don't overcomplicate it!

- You now need to **create an action plan** that you can follow. This action plan is essential to problem-solving as this is when you get to solve it.
- **Review the whole experience and look for lessons** that you have learned. This process will help you to fine-tune how you deal with problems.

Decision-making skills

- Always remember why you need to make the decision. It will stop you from overthinking things and going off track.
- Always double-check you are not showing any bias before you make a decision and check that you are thinking neutrally.
- Research the decision and get some information. It will allow you to consider different options.
- Think about the consequences of your decision. But also think about the consequences of indecision.
- Make an effort to find negative information and cases about the decision you are thinking of making. You will see your decision differently.
- Ask for the opinion of somebody else. It's always good to get another perspective on things. You might hear something you never thought of before.

An Interactive Element - Assertive Communication

You have come to the next interactive element of the book. In this section, you will learn how to use assertive communication. This form of communication enables you to stand up for yourself. At the same time, you also take into account the needs and wants of others. You can do this in a way without being passive or aggressive.

Assertiveness Exercise 1

Put some time aside to sit quietly and think about how you can be assertive. Think about a situation that you know will be challenging for you. **Visualize yourself as you are usually in this situation.** Then read these tips.

- ★ Always remember to respect yourself in any situation. Think about yourself expressing yourself but being respectful of the other person.
- ★ Calmly express your feelings and thoughts. Never shout at the other person, or threaten them. Also, don't use mind games, like being silent.
- ★ Think about what you will say to the person, and plan it so you know what words to use.
- ★ You can use the word, no. Don't feel bad about this. You can always come up with an alternative solution.

Now after reading the tips, visualize yourself back in this situation. Notice how differently you act. This visualization exercise can help you to gain confidence and use your assertiveness.

Assertiveness Exercise 2

Try doing these dummy scenario exercises to help you deal with different situations. Before writing down a response, think about your needs and wants.

Situation:
Some builders work on the house next door and start at 6 am. It keeps waking you up.

Write your assertive statement here:

Your Friend:

"Hi! Can you please lend me some money again? I swear I'll pay you back. I know I didn't last time, but this time will be different."

Write your assertive response here:

Situation:

You are at a restaurant, and the waiter has brought out the wrong dish. You asked for no tomatoes, and it had tomatoes.

Write your assertive statement here:

Your Partner:

"I know you have already arranged to see your friend. But I need you to cancel that and look after the kids, as my friend is coming to see me."

Write your assertive response here:

Summary

You have now come to the end of Chapter Six, and you should have a far greater understanding of how to use your interpersonal skills to build more healthy relationships. Work your way through the chapter slowly, and don't forget to try the assertiveness exercises to help you.

You can use all your new skills and start pushing yourself to greater heights. The next chapter will explain the importance of goal setting and give you strategies to go ahead and set goals for yourself. You can use these goals to realize your dreams and to create the life you always wanted.

07

DREAMS TO REALITY: PURPOSEFUL GOAL SETTING

> *"Successful people do things that the average person is not willing to do. They make sacrifices the average person is not willing to make. But the difference it makes is extraordinary."*
>
> —**BRIAN TRACY**

You want to be excellent at what you do, whether studying or advancing your career. But it can be hard to even think about achieving goals if you don't know how to set goals. This chapter is about goal setting and how you can finally plan and achieve your goals.

Goal setting can make your most exciting dreams come true.

Using the life skills you have already learned in this book, you can utilize them with your goals. Things that you never dreamt were possible are now available to you. It's not as easy as clicking your fingers, and your success will appear. It is best if you plan to achieve it. **Get ready to become a goal-setting machine!**

Why Goal Setting Is Useful For Young People

A goal is something that you are aiming to achieve. You can have goals for anything in your life. It could be to take the first step or next step in your career, to lose weight, to save money, to join a sports team, etc. Setting goals help you to have a sense of direction.

You can't move forward if you don't know where you are going.

When you start goal setting, you can focus your attention and behavior on your goal. Once goals are in place, they can also help you to make the right choices and decisions. All this focus is working together to achieve one thing - which is your goal.

Personal goal-setting tips

You might have tried to set goals in the past and failed. Or set unrealistic goals. As a young adult, this can be frustrating and sometimes demotivates you from trying again. Goal setting only works well when you know how to create and set goals that will work for you.

You know what is best for you when it comes to goal setting.

It's also important not to follow goal-setting advice from your parents and friends. Sure, you can listen to them for ideas. But when setting the actual goals themselves, they need to come from you. Because you know deep down what you want out of life, it's all about creating the best life possible for yourself.

Plus, once you start achieving your goals, the feeling of accomplishment is second to none. You will inspire yourself to go on and set more goals for yourself. There will be no stopping you as you will have the confidence to repeat your success again and again. This chapter will help you to set the best goals for yourself.

Consider your passions

Before you start setting goals, think about your passions. **You need to set goals that make you feel alive.** Setting goals because they sound good, or the same as your friends, will not help you in the long run. You don't want to achieve something that feels flat. Finding your purpose in life can help you set the right goals.

How to find your purpose

Finding your purpose is not some hippy-dippy thing in life. Once you know your purpose, it can help you formulate long-term plans with set goals. It's all about finding things that make you happy and then dedicating more time to them. **It's like the saying, "Do a job you love, and you'll never work a day in your life."**

When you start living a more purposeful life, it can boost your physical health and mental fitness. It can reduce the risk of chronic diseases, and many studies show that you live longer. It's important to note that your purpose can change in life. Whatever it is right now, it might not be the same ten years from now.

Here are twelve tips to help you find your purpose:

1. **Start to develop a growth mindset**
   If you have a growth mindset, you constantly want to grow and become a better version of yourself.

2. **Make a personal vision statement**
   It can help you to find balance and manage stress in your life. You can identify your core values and know what is important to you.

3. **Help Others**

    It could be charity work or simply helping somebody. By helping others, you can help yourself. It enhances your sense of self and gives you purpose in life.

4. **Remember to practice gratitude**

    Studies find that gratitude activates reward responses in the brain. When you focus on gratitude, it can strengthen your sense of purpose.

5. **Flip your pain into your purpose**

    If you have a major challenge in life, how you overcome it could be your purpose. You could share this with others and inspire them.

6. **Look at your passions and interests**

    Your passions can be a strong indicator of where your purpose lies. If you are stuck, ask people who know you what passions you show.

7. **Use the community spirit**

    When you connect with others, you can feel a sense of purpose. Become an active community member, giving you a sense of purpose.

8. **Look out for people who inspire you**

    Try to spend time with people who inspire you. These positive people are purpose-driven and can help you realize your true purpose.

9. **Read as many books as you can**

    It doesn't matter if you prefer a paperback or reading on a kindle. Non-fiction can help you acquire knowledge, and fiction can improve critical thinking.

10. **Join one of your passionate causes**

    Everybody has a cause that makes them feel passionate. What is yours? Whatever it is, get involved and start driving that purpose in your life.

11. **Accept who you are**

    Be kind to yourself and accept your limitations instead of being hard on yourself. It will help you to feel more connected and find your purpose in life.

12. **Spend time on self-care**

    Relax and give yourself a break. It can help to relax your brain, so you are more creative. When you are relaxed, you might think more about your life purpose.

Set goals you can control

When it comes to goal setting, make sure you control them. If you can't use control over your goals, you will not achieve them. Whatever goals you set, you need to check them regularly and monitor the results. You have a higher chance of success by managing and controlling your goals.

Imagine your future

When the going gets tough, the tough get going! On those days when it feels like your goals are far away, imagine your future. In the future, you will have achieved your goals and will be enjoying a better life. Bear this in mind on those tough days, and keep going.

Tips For Setting Goals At Work

Here are a couple of simple tips for setting team goals when you are at work:

Brainstorm

Before you write down any goal in a team environment, it's best to brainstorm it first. Get the whole team involved so that everybody can contribute with ideas. Write them all down and then decide together which goal is best for the team.

Ask Searching Questions

Discuss together the purpose of your group goal. Make sure you have a relaxed atmosphere, so people feel comfortable. Ask searching questions like, "What does success look like to us?", "What are we doing?" and "Where do we want to be?."

How To Achieve Your Goals

To achieve your goals, you need to set yourself up for success. You don't want to fail at your goals and feel negative about yourself. It's all about creating the best situation for yourself to excel and experience success.

Here are twelve ways in which you can help you achieve your goals:

1. **Use SMART goals**
   You might have heard this before and wondered what it was about. It would help if you created **SMART** goals.

   - ★ **Specific** - Be very clear and not vague. It must be clear what the end goal is, so you don't lose focus.
   - ★ **Measurable** - To reach your goal, you must declare a set amount/completion of something/target.
   - ★ **Attainable** - The target must be within your reach. You can use data and research to set proper attainable goals.

- ★ **Relevant** - Make sure the goal is relevant to what you are doing. Otherwise, it is completely pointless. Check that the goal sits with your needs and wants.
- ★ **Time-bound** - Set a time when the goal should be complete. It also needs to be set for the right time. Not too far ahead and not too short.

Here are some smart goals examples, so you can see how it works in practice.

<u>Example 1</u>
If you wanted a better relationship with your brother, it could work as follows:

Specific: I want a better relationship with my brother.
Measurable: I will contact my brother twice a week by text and meet once a week.
Attainable: I have more free time, so I have time to meet with him.
Relevant: I can improve relationships with my family members.
Time-bound: I want to complete this by the end of the month.

<u>Example 2</u>
If you want to create better communication at work:

Specific: I will help my team to communicate more effectively with each other.
Measurable: I will create more slack channels.
Attainable: All my colleagues can use technology.
Relevant: There will be more projects soon, so this will help.
Time-bound: I will send slack invites tomorrow.

2. **Write Your Goals Down**

    It's easy to think about goals and not take any action. Make sure you write down your goals so that they are there in black and white. You can do this on paper, mobile, tablet, laptop, or PC. **It makes them more real!**

3. **Make Sure Your Goals Are Visible**

    Once you have written your goals, make sure they are somewhere you can see them regularly. If they are personal goals, you could put them in your bathroom. Put them on a bulletin board if they are for your team at work.

4. **Breakdown The Goals**

    You can make the goals easier by breaking them down into smaller ones. It will make the big goal seem less daunting. **A "goal ladder" is a great way to do this.** You can put the smaller goals on each rung of the ladder.

5. **Create A Plan**

    You know where you want to go, but you need the plan to get there. Write down all the little things you need to do to get there. You can cross them off when you have achieved them.

6. **Do It**

    Less talk and more action! Now it's time to get going and start moving towards your goals. It doesn't matter how small your actions are as long as you do something to achieve your goal.

7. **Keep Your Feet On The Ground**

    It's easy to get caught up in wanting to achieve a goal. Don't let it become an obsession. **You don't want to burn yourself out.** Take your time and keep things in perspective.

8. **Identify Obstacles**

    There will always be obstacles in whatever you do in life. It is also the same for goals. Prepare yourself for obstacles that can happen so that you can handle them when they do.

9. **Make Yourself Accountable**

    Trying to do a goal by yourself can sometimes feel lonely. Let a friend know what you are doing so they can keep track and hold you accountable. If it's a team goal at work, your team could share it with another team, so you have some encouragement.

10. **Review And Adapt**

    Review your goals and see how you performed. Don't be hard on yourself if you don't achieve everything you want. The goalposts might have changed. Alternatively, the goal might have been unattainable. If so, adjust it for next time.

Why Time management Is Important In Goal Setting

Everybody wants to achieve their goals as quickly as possible because your goal is something you want to achieve. But rushing things and trying to make them happen quicker will not be good for your goals. It will put you under pressure.

As you get older, it starts to feel like you need more time. You find you have far more things to do each day. It can feel challenging to juggle all the balls and try not to drop any of them! Luckily, there are things you can do to make it a lot easier for yourself.

Effective Time Management Strategies

Here are some effective time management strategies that you can use to help you:

Don't Multitask

Studies have shown that if you keep swapping between tasks, it can decrease your productivity. Also, you can lose focus and start making mistakes. Stick to one thing at a time to ensure you are both productive and effective.

Take Breaks

Taking a break is a necessity. Don't think taking a break slows you down. Breaks help to refresh you, and you can go back to work with more focus. Make sure you do something relaxing during your break to switch off mentally.

Track What Takes Up All Your Time

For one whole week, note everything you do every 15 minutes. It is an easy way for you to see what you are spending your time on. You can then eliminate things that are too time-consuming for you.

Ask For Help If You Need It

Don't suffer in silence. If you need help, ask for it. You might feel you have bitten off more than you can chew. There is no point plodding on like this. Ask for help to share the work and make things easier for yourself.

Organize

Try to plan and organize yourself. If you have tasks, you do every week, put them in your calendar or a diary. You can then see what time you have free and where you can move things around when you are busy.

How To Organize Everything In Your Busy Life

You're enjoying your new life and the freedom of living by yourself. But sometimes, it can get a bit hectic and overwhelming. So what can you do to organize your busy life? Here are ten tips to help you arrange your time and have some balance in your busy life.

1. Build A Routine For Yourself With Good Habits

You might have fallen into the habit of looking at your social media a few times each day. While staying in touch with your friends and family is great, it can sometimes be distracting. Create a new routine that takes this into account. Also, limit binge-watching on Netflix and remember to take proper breaks.

- ★ Limit your total amount of time on social media each day
- ★ Have a set amount of television time
- ★ Arrange 30 minutes each day to take a break and relax

2. Plan Your Week Ahead

Take your organizational skills to the next level. Sit down at the end of each week and plan for the next week. You can use apps like Asana or Trello to help you. They both have a free version. It will help you stay organized and on track with all your daily tasks.

- ★ Sign up for Asana or Trello and arrange your next week ahead
- ★ At the end of the week, check how you did it and "tweak" it for next week
- ★ Be critical with your tasks and eliminate anything unnecessary

3. Do Things That Come Naturally To You

It's easy to look at your friends and celebrities and think they are doing things better than you. However, this is not the case. Everybody needs to do something that comes naturally to them. Don't force things on yourself that you don't like. Make a point of doing things that you like or even love doing.

- ★ Think about what you love to eat and make sure you eat it once a week

- ★ Say no to work you don't like doing and offer to do something else instead
- ★ Be honest with family and friends and tell them when you are too tired to visit

4. Don't Create Unrealistic Plans

If you want to start going to the gym and working out to get healthy, be realistic about what you can do. Don't tell yourself you will go three times a week, do it the 1st week and then start dropping off. It will demotivate you and make you feel worse. Think about what you can realistically do and do that.

- ★ Decide how many times you will realistically exercise every work
- ★ Decide how many times you can eat out every month and stick to it
- ★ Go to bed earlier three times every week instead of every night

5. Look For Some Balance In Your Life

You are the same as everyone else when searching for the perfect life/work balance. It will never be possible to have it 100% of the time. But you can take steps to balance it as best as you can. Be critical about what you are doing in your work and "normal" life, and see where you can improve things.

- ★ Start meditating or create a gratitude journal
- ★ Spend some alone time with a good book
- ★ Go for a walk to relax and destress

6. Prioritize In The Right Way

When you start prioritizing things in your life, everything can feel so much better. Once again, being critical of yourself and your life would be best.

Do you need to binge-watch the new Netflix series? Do you have to go to 3 different grocery stores because you like other brands?

- ★ Make things you love to do a priority in your life.
- ★ Prioritize activities that make you feel energized
- ★ Take on new opportunities that help you learn and grow

7. Make Your Life Simple

You might have an obsession with downloading the latest app. It can get to the point where you have an app for everything. While these apps might be helpful, they can sometimes make you feel more stressed. The same for your home. Is it minimalistic, or do you have stuff everywhere?

- ★ Spend a full day decluttering your home and get rid of "the stuff"
- ★ Remove apps from your mobile that you don't use often
- ★ Clear workspace, so nothing is distracting you

8. Measure Your Life

Like you did with your SMART goals, you can also measure your life and see how it is doing. Give yourself a weekly review. Sit down and assess your progress. It can highlight problem areas for you, and you can also enjoy thinking about your achievements. It can help to refocus on your efforts and do better the next week

- ★ Refine your daily to-do lists and update them if they feel out of date
- ★ Assess personal relationships and put more energy into them if they need it
- ★ Look at your morning and night schedules. Can you improve them?

9. Use Apps And Outsource Work

You've got rid of the apps that you are not using. But that doesn't mean you can't use some to help you. You need to find the ones that are most beneficial to you. Likewise, when it comes to your workload, outsource some tasks to somebody else and save valuable time.

- ★ Find an app to help you with budgeting and use it daily
- ★ Use a virtual assistant to help you with administrative tasks
- ★ Do your grocery shopping online and let them deliver it to you

10. Try Something Different

There is nothing to stop you from trying something new. It can bring a new perspective to your life. You don't have to do the same thing every day. Be a rebel and break the routine! It can help you breathe fresh air into your world to open your mind to new challenges and goals.

- ★ Look for a new job
- ★ Go out and make some new friends
- ★ Find a new hobby
- ★ Workout at at a different gym

An Interactive Element - Goal-Setting Worksheet

You have come to the next interactive element of the book. **You can use the goal-setting worksheet in this section to create your goals.** Don't be afraid to experiment and try a few small ones first. You can then move on to more challenging goals once you have had some practice.

GOAL-SETTING WORKSHEET

Name:

Goal start date:

Goal completion date:

The goal I want to achieve is:

....

....

The five steps I need to take to reach my goal:
1)
2)
3)
4)
5)

The three things that will help me achieve my goal:
1)
2)
3)

How I will know that I have reached my goal:

....

....

Fill in this goal-setting worksheet and use it for your 1st goal. You can then replicate the form yourself and continue setting new goals. The worksheet is a model, so you can always change the form to make it more appropriate for yourself. You should add new sections depending on the type of goal that you set yourself.

Good luck, and enjoy achieving your goals!

Summary

You have now come to the end of Chapter Seven. After reading this chapter and using the interactive goal-setting worksheet, you should feel confident setting goals. Goal setting is an integral part of adulthood and can help you achieve the things you want by yourself. It can feel very empowering!

In the next chapter, which is the last one of the book, you will learn how to put a plan in place for your career. Planning your career as a young adult can help you be more successful later in life. You'll learn even more about yourself and can create a proper career plan to help you achieve your career goals.

08

THE CAREER BLUEPRINT: CRAFTING YOUR PATH TO SUCCESS

"The difference between great people and everyone else is that great people create their lives actively, while everyone else is created by their lives, passively waiting to see where life takes them next. The difference between the two is the difference between living fully and just existing."

—**MICHAEL E. GERBER**

The quote above defines how important career planning is for young adults. You might have moments when you feel down and anxious about your career. It's hard not to feel pressure from your family or society to perform well at work and have an established career.

Career planning is the key to career success.

In the last chapter, you learned how to set goals. You can use these new skills to help you forge your career path. You might have already started your career and are looking to take it to the next level. Whatever stage you are at, planning it out will be the key to achieving success in your chosen career.

It's natural to want to excel in your career.

This final chapter will explain the importance of career planning at a young age. You will also learn about different strategies you can use to help you choose and ultimately succeed in your career. Before we get into it, you need to know the difference between a career and a job. Read on to find out more!

The Difference Between A Career And A Job

You might already be under the impression that your job is your work and that it is your career. But a career is precious. It can make a huge difference in your life as you get older. In reality, a job is something that you do to earn money. A career is a long-term commitment. It is something that you build towards and work on daily.

A career is so much more than a job.

A job is only a role that you do. In contrast, a career consists of several roles, work experience, education, and different paths you take to achieve career goals. It's normal for people to have a job to pay the bills. But if you want to achieve and work towards a career, you must put career goals in place.

Here are some key differences between working at a job and focusing on a career:

- A job gives you short-term funds to pay bills. A career provides long-term financial security as you build skills, learn more and advance your career.

- Jobs can be insecure, especially during a recession. If you have a career with experience, skills, and qualifications, it can act as a safety net.
- You have more chances of earning higher pay when you have a career. As you progress in your career, you earn more and learn more.
- If you have passion for your chosen career, it can make your job feel rewarding. You will feel challenged and motivated daily.

Why You Need To Plan Your Career While You're Young

Deciding what you want to do in your career can put some young adults into a panic. In high school, there is a big push for you to make the decision. But if you haven't thought about it before, sometimes it is hard to pin down the right career path. You might worry about making the wrong decision.

Knowing where you are going is always better than feeling lost.

The digital age has now brought more opportunities for young people. You don't always have to go into traditional career roles like a doctor, an engineer, a lawyer, etc. There are now more unconventional roles that you can choose to do. Finding the right career path can be confusing with all these new options.

Plan your career and take the confusion out of your future.

Planning is the cornerstone of any successful career. Planning when you are younger allows you to look at all your hobbies and interests. You can spend time researching what is out there and matches your specific areas of interest. Here are six tips to inspire you to plan your career while you are still young:

- ★ **Create A Niche For Yourself**

    If you realize that you like a particular subject, you can plan to educate yourself in this area. Over time you will create a niche for yourself that will help you to advance your career.

- ★ **You Can Channel Your Energy**

    When you are younger, it feels like you have limitless energy. Instead of spreading this energy everywhere, you can focus your energy on what you enjoy. It will help you to gain solid working knowledge in one area.

- ★ **You Can Gain Insight With An Internship**

    You can do a paid or unpaid internship in the subject that interests you. It will give you a wealth of knowledge and insight into that field. You might not like it when you do it, and it helps you change your career path before it is too late.

- ★ **You Can Get To Grips With Technology**

    Due to technology, the current and new generations that enter the marketplace have broader perspectives on situations. You can make yourself as technologically adept as possible and learn as many complementary skills as possible.

- ★ **Career Planning Gives Clear Directions**

    Spending time on career exploration can help you discover your strengths and weaknesses. You can then focus on your strengths and tie these to your future career goals. It will help improve your performance and guide you to the right career.

- ★ **Get Coaching From An Expert**

    It doesn't matter how old you are. You can work with a coach or career expert. It can help you to create clear career goals and get unbiased advice about your career options. You can gain a clear advantage over your future career competitors.

How To Choose The Right Career For You

The top three things people care about the most are their family, health, and work. Therefore, taking the right career path is essential to your life. Learning everything you need for your chosen career path can take weeks, months, or even years. You might change your course several times as you work through your career.

NB, There are activities for reflection later in the interactive element of this chapter.

The Career Planning Process

Here are seven steps that you can use to help you choose the right career. In the interactive element section, there are further career reflection activities later in the chapter.

Step 1: Self-Assessment

Before making any important decisions about your career, it is best to think about your life. You might have a good idea of what kind of work environment you like. The type of work you enjoy and the type of people you want to work with. It gives you a basic idea of the type of career that would suit you.

While you are in this self-assessment phase, ask yourself the following questions and write down your answers. Try to be as thorough as you can. NB, It's best to write down the first thought that comes into your mind instead of overthinking your responses.

- What soft skills do I have? (e.g., communication, time management, and problem-solving skills.)
- What technical skills do I have? (e.g., data analytics, languages, and research.)
- What type of personality do I have? (e.g., confident, loyal, quiet)
- What interests me? (e.g., design, technology, writing)

Step 2: Career Exploration

Once you have answered these questions, you can move on to career exploration. You now need to gather information about a potential career. This gathering process is an essential part of career planning. Remember to keep notes and reference where you found the information.

There are several different things you can do to find the information you need:

- Read everything you can about different careers.
- Talk to people who are already doing it to get an objective perspective

- Enrol in a course for the subject you are interested in to see what it is like
- Do a short internship to get hands-on experience so you can check it out

Top Tip

Only do a course or an internship if you already have a reasonably strong interest in that topic, as they can be time-consuming.

Step 3: Targeting

After investigating several different careers, you are now ready to target one and focus on that. You might have reduced your original choices down to three clear favorites. If you still can't decide, you might need to do more research on the ones you have left.

Once you have all the information, you need to use it carefully to help you make the right decision. You can sit down and evaluate your potential outcome depending on each career choice. Does it feel right for you? Can you see yourself doing that career five years from now? You can select the right one for you.

Step 4: Career Preparation

Now that you have made your career decision, you need to start preparing for your future career. You need to find out what type of experience you need and how to enter this field. Also, what qualifications do you need to do this? Do you have some already, or will you need to educate yourself further?

Find out what extra education you need and how you can do it, e.g., courses, internships, specific training, etc. You won't be able to accomplish it all at once, so you can use your goal-setting skills here. Set up some individual career goals. Use short and long-term goals so you can check your progress.

Step 5: Marketing Yourself

You have pinpointed your career and are taking the necessary steps to get there. But you are not guaranteed a job will be available when you graduate or finish your last course or internship. A degree or other experience and qualifications will open doors for you, but to get into the door, you need to market yourself.

Traditional methods of job hunting are things like:

- ★ Sending resumes to job adverts
- ★ Using an employment agency
- ★ Participating in on-campus recruiting

Now, there are more non-traditional approaches that people are using to get jobs. This type of job hunting is known as networking. Here are some examples of networking:

- ★ Reaching out to friends
- ★ Contacting people from your alumni
- ★ Approaching professional association members
- ★ Using business networking sites like LinkedIn

Studies show that finding a new job can take up to six months. Six months is a long time, and job hunting can feel like a full-time job. You can increase your chances of success by combining traditional and more modern job-seeking strategies.

Step 6: Career Management

Hopefully, you are now working in the position that you had your heart set on. Remember that only some jobs can give you everything you need. Use your positions to help to educate yourself further and progress. Also, don't forget to have an excellent work-life balance, so you stay stress-free.

Working in an organization or for yourself differs from going to school or university. In educational institutions, you must learn and then do assessments and exams. You have to produce results in a work environment, sometimes without any direction or feedback.

Keep on top of your career ambitions and monitor your progress. Not every job lasts for a lifetime as it used to years ago. You have to learn to be flexible in the job market space. Always look for new opportunities to grow and learn so you can keep your career advancing. **When you are ready to move on, go back to Step One!**

How To Succeed In Your Early Years At Work

You might feel nervous in your early years of work as you think you lack the skills and experience to do well. However, times are changing, and it's not always about how many years of experience you have. There are a few things you can do to help you succeed in your first years at work. Use these four tips to help you:

Be emotionally intelligent

You can't learn how to be emotionally intelligent, but being able to read a room or somebody's emotions can help you immensely. If you don't use emotional intelligence, you might come across as unprofessional or end up in awkward situations.

The section in Chapter Six helped you improve your emotional intelligence. You can also observe how your co-workers and boss interact with each other. If you watch these interactions, you can pick up cues to help you. Don't forget to look for body language and listen to the tone when people speak.

Be personable, not personal

Wanting to create a good relationship with your co-workers is great, but you have to make ensure you don't cross the line. You can show an interest in them and their personal lives to help build a rapport, but you have to know when is enough. You shouldn't see them 24/7 and know everything about each other.

Don't discuss hot topics that could lead to an argument or future tension. Keep away from areas such as religion, politics, and sex. Also, your co-worker doesn't need to know what you did when you were drunk. Likewise, talking about money can make people feel uncomfortable and is best avoided.

Learn to manage up

Building a strong, healthy relationship with your manager can be mutually beneficial. Try to find out what your manager values in their personal and professional life. Find out what that they want to accomplish and help them get there. You can do things to make the job easier for them and, at the same time, express your goals.

You should also remember to record your achievements and successes at work. Sometimes when organizations are so busy, it can feel like a never-ending cycle of projects. If you have done well in a project, don't forget to "blow your trumpet" now and then. It reminds your manager what you have done and can do.

Plan ahead

There is a lot of talking about planning in this book. But it is there for a good reason. Without planning, you are like a ship lost at sea with no direction. Planning helps to keep you on track so you can get where you want to go. In this case, it will help you to achieve your career goals.

Keep track of where you are in your position and your career path. It will help you stay motivated and encourage you to keep going. Always remember where you want to be in the future and stick to your plan. Don't forget to communicate your career goals to your manager, and they will help you to get there.

What Is A Career Development Plan?

A career development plan is an action plan that you can use for your career to guide you. You can use it to create an exact roadmap for your career. A typical career development plan has four main areas:

The starting point
This point details exactly where you are right now in your career.

The destination
This area explains where you want to go in your career.

The gap
This section details the obstacles you must overcome to reach your destination.

The route
In the route section, you detail how you will close the gap to reach your destination.

How To Create A Career Development Plan For Yourself

You don't need to hire an expensive career coach to create a development plan for you. Here are the five steps you need to follow to create one. Follow each step carefully and fill in as much information as possible, as you work your way through.

1. Identify the current position in your career

The first step is to identify where you are in your career. It's also a great step to reflect on your current skills and strengths. These will have probably changed as you have been working through this book. You might be pleasantly surprised to see how you have grown so far.

To identify where you are right now, ask yourself the following questions:

- What kinds of natural skills and talents do I have?
- What is my work experience so far?
- Do I have a calling in life?
- What energizes me, and what makes me feel tired?
- What motivates and excites me when I do work?
- Do I prefer working in a group or working by myself?

Once you have answered these questions, you can note your current position in your career field. For example, if you have finished graduate school, you might want to do more education. Also, don't forget to detail where you currently sit on your career ladder.

2. Identify the destination for your career

In the next step, you are identifying your destination so you know where you need to go in your career. Here are three things you can do to complete this next step:

- **Conduct a brainstorming session**
  Don't be shy and let your mind run rampant. Think about your dream career. What is your ultimate career goal? For example, if you want to be a CEO of a company, write that in your plan.

- **Think about specific goals**
  To help you get to your destination, you need specific goals. Using the goal-setting techniques in the last chapter. Write down short-term career goals leading to a long-term goal.

- **The next five to 10 years**
  It's a question you get asked in interviews, but it's important. Where do you want to be five to ten years from now? Write down if it is the same job, a higher role, or a different career altogether.

3. Do a gap analysis

The first two steps will help you better understand your skills and your different career options. You can now assess to work out how to get to your target destination.

- **Research your career goals**
  Using the career goals that you made previously, find job listings for the jobs you want. Ensure the jobs match your experience and skills and fit with your future career ambitions.

- **Check your qualifications**
  Use your list of experience and skills and rate them against the requirements. A rating system from 1 to 5, with five being the highest, will work for this. You will see which areas need more improvement.

- **Look for gaps and patterns**
  By grouping common skills and experiences, you will notice different patterns - ones with a solid background and others that need development. Focus on the gaps and list what you need to do.

4. Create a career development plan

Now you have a detailed list of the education, experience, and skills you need to develop to advance your career. You can create a concrete plan with this information.

- **Set small goals for yourself**
  Start by creating a list of things you need to do to achieve little goals. For example, if you need to learn software, sign up for a course, ask a colleague about it, or practice using it at work.

- **Set a timeline**
  Using your goal-setting skills again, start devising ways to create short and long-term goals. Don't forget to ensure your goals are SMART so you have a higher chance of achieving them.

- **Use task deadlines**
  You can create deadlines to ensure you are held accountable for each task in your goals. You can allocate a "Start by" and "Complete by" date for every task.

5. Track your progress and be open to changing your plan

Now that you have a career development plan, you need to look after it so that it works for you. Here are three things you can do to ensure that your plan works.

- **Track your progress**
  Remember to check that you are meeting your completion dates set in Step Four. You don't need to be obsessive. Checking them sporadically throughout the year should be enough to make sure you're on track.

- **Use milestones**
  There are different ways you can measure how well you are doing in your career plan - things like landing a new job, having a positive performance review, gaining a promotion, or winning an award.

- **Update your goals**
  The world is constantly changing, and so are you. For example, you might fall into a completely different career, or you might have to move to another country. You can still take control by updating your goals.

An Interactive Element - Knowing Yourself On A Deeper Level

You have come to the last interactive element of the book. **You can use the career planning worksheet in this section to help you plan your career.** Don't forget you can also adapt the worksheet to how you see fit, so it can better match your circumstances.

CAREER PLANNING WORKSHEET

Name:

Date:

My personality:

1) How do I like to interact with the world around me? Would I class myself as an introvert or extrovert?
   ....
   ....

2) How do I view the world around me? Would I class myself as intuitive or sensing?
   ....
   ....

3) How do I make decisions? Do I feel things, or am I a deep thinker?
   ....
   ....

4) How do I like to organize my life? Do I perceive things, or do I judge things?
   ....
   ....

My values:

My top five personal, lifestyle, and workplace values are:

1)

2)

3)

4)

5)

My strengths:

1) What are the skills I enjoy using?

　...

　...

2) What skills do I not have would like to develop?

　...

　...

My aptitude:

1) Which courses have I performed well in?

　...

　...

2) What comes naturally to me?

....

....

3) What does not come naturally to me?

....

....

My obstacles:

1) What are my internal obstacles?

....

....

2) What are my external obstacles?

....

....

CONCLUSION

Congratulations, you made it!

You have come to the end of the book and should feel a sense of accomplishment. Your brain is full of valuable information to help you as you move into adulthood. Fill up your chest with pride for achieving your first goal of finishing this book.

Remember, this is only the beginning of your adulthood journey.

Adulting may be full of challenges, but that's life, even from the day you are born. The best thing you can do is equip yourself with the skills you need to get there. By reading this book, you have given yourself a significant headstart in your life.

You will make mistakes along the way but don't lose heart. Always remember that learning takes a lifetime. Choose to learn from your mistakes so you can grow wiser and stronger.

Adulthood does not happen overnight, and this book will guide you.

You can now feel comfortable in the kitchen and know how to buy, store and cook your food. You can also handle any emergencies in your home or when you are out driving. Additionally, you have the repair and maintenance skills to fix things at home and save money - and a home maintenance checklist to help you every year.

You understand your physical and mental health's importance and how to look after it. The interactive element offered you some fantastic mindfulness exercises you can use throughout your life. You also learned crucial money skills and how to manage money to gain financial stability and freedom.

You have the interpersonal skills to help you make yourself understood and to build healthy personal and professional relationships. Also, you better understand how to handle problems and make clear decisions. The assertiveness exercises helped take things further with your communication skills.

And finally, you learned how to create and set goals to help you realize your dreams. Plus, how to use your new goal-setting skills to help you plan a successful career. With the interactive element and using all the tips, you could find the best career path for your future.

Use your new skills to create the life you always wanted.

All these skills are now inside you and ready to use. You can apply these essential life skills to your life's different areas. You will start seeing the results immediately and can keep learning and moving forward. Every step will lead to the next one, and your confidence will shine.

I wish you all the best on your exciting journey ahead!

Spread The Word

Pushing Confidently Forward In Your Life

Now you have learned all the essential life skills to help you be a success in whatever you decide to do. You can care and share the wisdom from this book to help people just like you. Let's create a new generation that can ride the wave of success!

By leaving your honest opinion of this book on Amazon, you'll show other young adults where they can find information on skills they need to move into adulthood.

LEAVE A REVIEW!

I appreciate your help. You are helping other young people gain the life skills they need to be independent and grow into their best lives.

You can also check out my other book "Conquering Discipline" to help boost your personal development even further.

Feel free to connect with me at contact@nmhill.com

INNER CIRCLE

Would you like to be a part of my inner circle?

I have nothing to giveaway if you decide to sign-up.

There is no free ebook or worksheet which most likely you don't want anyway.

What I can promise is that by being a part of my inner circle you will receive random emails from me from time to time.

Some will be personal development related, some will be personal and some will just try and make you laugh or at the very least put a smile on your face!

I promise not to bombard you daily with emails to clog up your inbox. As a reader of my book and fellow human, I value and care about you too much.

You can unsubscribe at any time you've had enough.

Now, I'm guessing you know what to do with the below QR Code.

9 EASY RECIPES YOU CAN DO YOURSELF

Here are nine simple recipes that you can make for yourself. Start with the breakfast ones first and work your way up to the lunch and dinner ones. Once you can do these recipes easily, start experimenting with new ones. You can even begin to make some up for yourself. **Enjoy your cooking, chef!**

Breakfast Recipes

Try these three breakfast recipes that have five ingredients or less.

Cheese and Onion Waffle Sandwich

Ingredients

1 large egg
1 green onion (chopped)
2 low-fat, multigrain waffles
1 tablespoon of cheddar cheese (shredded and reduced-fat)
Sliced tomato

Directions

- Whisk together the egg and onion in a bowl. Cook the egg and keep stirring it until there is no liquid egg left.
- Get the waffles ready as per the package directions. Put one waffle on a plate and then top it with scrambled egg, cheese, and tomato. Put another waffle on top.

Cinnamon Applesauce Pancakes

Ingredients

1 cup of pancake mix (buttermilk)
1 teaspoon of cinnamon (ground)
1 cup applesauce (chunky cinnamon)
¼ cup of water
Butter and maple syrup

Directions

- Mix the pancake mix and the cinnamon.
- Then, add the applesauce and water and stir until it is moist.
- Pour the batter, a ¼ of a cup at a time, onto a greased hot griddle. When bubbles appear on the top, turn it over.
- Keep cooking until the second side is golden brown.
- Then serve with butter and syrup.

Berries In Yoghurt Cream

Ingredients

1 and a half cups of plain yogurt
Half a cup of packed brown sugar
5 cups of mixed berries
125g of cream

Directions

- Put the yogurt in a large bowl and whisk in the cream.
- Sprinkle with brown sugar, but don't stir it.
- Cover it and put it in the fridge for 3 hours.
- Divide the mixture in ten dessert bowls, then put the berries on top.

Lunch Recipes

Here are three lunch recipes you can make in ten minutes or less.

Arugula Tuna Avocado Salad

Ingredients

A tin of tuna
1 avocado
2-3 handfuls of baby arugula
1-3 teaspoons of olive oil
A squeeze of lemon
Cherry tomatoes (halved)
Cucumber (slices)
Sliced red onion
Olives

Directions

- Put all the ingredients into a bowl and gently toss. Enjoy!

Creamy Spaghetti

Ingredients

Regular or wholegrain pasta
Cream cheese
Parmesan cheese
Garlic
Olive Oil
Salt and Pepper

Optional

Half a cup of fresh chopped spinach (10g)

Directions

- Cook pasta according to the package directions.
- Gently cook the garlic in the olive oil for a few minutes in a pan.
- Add the cream cheese and parmesan cheese to the pan and stir well. (You can also add ham and spinach here if you desire).
- Drain the pasta and add it to the pan.
- Add salt and pepper to taste.

Margarita Naan Bread Pizza

Ingredients

2 Naans
Tomato sauce
Garlic powder
Italian mixed herbs
Sliced fresh mozzarella
Fresh basil (handful)
Salt and pepper
Olive oil

Directions

- Put the oven's broiler on the high setting and move the oven rack to the top part of the oven.
- Put the naan bread on a large or two small baking sheets.
- On each naan, put a layer of tomato sauce.
- Sprinkle each naan with garlic powder and Italian mixed herbs.
- Add a few slices of Mozzarella cheese to each naan bread.
- Fill in any gaps with basil.
- Season with salt and pepper.
- Broil for around 5 minutes or until the cheese is slightly brown at the edges.
- When finished, add a drizzle of olive oil and serve immediately.

Dinner Recipes

Here are three dinner recipes that take thirty minutes or less to cook.

Cashew Chicken

Ingredients

2 Chicken (boneless and skinless breast or thighs)
1 tablespoon of Vegetable oil
Salt to taste
1 tablespoon of cornstarch
2 Red peppers
A few roasted cashew nuts

Sauce: Teaspoon of Soy sauce, a teaspoon of rice vinegar, ¼ cup of chicken broth, a pinch of brown sugar, a teaspoon of fresh ginger, a teaspoon of sesame oil and a teaspoon of cornstarch.

Directions

- Cut the chicken into 1" cubes. Put one tablespoon of oil, salt, and cornstarch in a mixing bowl. Stir well to coat the chicken.
- Cook the chicken with 1 tablespoon of oil in a large skill with medium-high heat. Do this for about 5-6 minutes until the chicken is golden brown.
- Take the chicken out and put the vegetables in. Cook for about 2-3 minutes.
- Make the sauce in a mixing bowl using the ingredients listed above.
- Add the sauce to the vegetables and simmer for 3-4 minutes.
- Add the chicken and the cashew nuts. Cook for about 1 minute.
- Serve with rice.

Parmesan Crumb Fish

Ingredients

2 white fish fillets (about 150g each with no skin)
2 tablespoons of mustard
Olive oil spray
Salt and pepper

To make the breadcrumb:

½ cup breadcrumbs
1 tablespoon of parsley (chopped)
⅓ cup of parmesan cheese
1 garlic clove (minced)
1 tablespoon of oil
Salt to taste

Directions

- Preheat the grill or broiler.
- Mix the breadcrumb ingredients.
- Sprinkle both sides of the fish with salt and pepper.
- Spread the mustard on the top of each fillet (only on one side).
- Press the mustard into the breadcrumb mixture.
- Then spray it with oil.
- Warm some oil in the skillet until it is hot and then place the fillets in the pan for about 5-6 minutes until it is golden. Keep rotating the fish.
- Alternatively bake in the oven at 390F for 10-12 minutes.

Garlic Shrimp Zoodles

Ingredients

2 medium-sized zucchinis
¾ pounds of peeled shrimp
1 tablespoon of olive oil
Zest of a lemon
3-4 cloves of garlic
Salt and pepper to taste
Fresh parsley (chopped)

Directions

- Cut the zucchini into spirals.
- Add the olive oil and lemon juice zest in a skillet on medium heat.
- Add the shrimp when the skillet is ready. Cook the shrimp for one minute on each side.
- Add the garlic and cook for another minute.
- Add the zucchini and stir for 2-3 minutes.
- Season with salt and pepper, and sprinkle the parsley on top.

REFERENCES

Chapter One

Catalina, C. (2021, November 17). *9 Reasons Why You Should Learn How To Cook*. Daydream Into Reality. https://www.daydreamintoreality.com/reasons-cook

Miranda, R. (2020, April 1). *Grocery Shopping For The First Time? We Have Tips For Buying Meat, Veggies, And Fruits*. Yummy. https://www.yummy.ph/lessons/prepping/first-time-grocery-shopping-tips-a00249-20200401-lfrm

Food safety. (2022, May 19). https://www.who.int/news-room/fact-sheets/detail/food-safety

How to Store Vegetables to Keep them Fresh - Unlock Food. (n.d.). https://www.unlockfood.ca/en/Articles/Cooking-Food-Preparation/How-to-store-vegetables-to-keep-them-fresh

Cookist, C. (2020, November 16). *How to preserve fresh meat: rules and tips to make it last long*. Cookist.com. https://www.cookist.com/how-to-preserve-fresh-meat-rules-and-tips-to-make-it-last-long/

Understanding Expiration Dates: How do I know when my food's gone bad? (2021, January 14). www.heart.org. https://www.heart.org/en/

healthy-living/healthy-eating/cooking-skills/storing/understanding-expiration-dates-how-do-i-know-when-my-foods-gone-bad

How to Store Fruit to Keep them Fresh - Unlock Food. (n.d.). https://www.unlockfood.ca/en/Articles/Cooking-Food-Preparation/How-to-store-fruit-to-keep-them-fresh.aspx

It's Usually Safe to Eat Food Past the Expiration Date—Here's How to Know When It's Ok. (2023, January 30). Real Simple. https://www.realsimple.com/food-recipes/shopping-storing/food/food-expiration-dates-guidelines-chart

Food Product Dating. (2019, October 2). USDA Food Inspection and Safety Service. https://www.fsis.usda.gov/food-safety/safe-food-handling-and-preparation/food-safety-basics/food-product-dating

Institute of Food Technologists (IFT). (2015, April 15). *The Difference between "Use-By" "Sell-By" and "Best-By" Dates.* https://www.newswise.com/articles/the-difference-between-use-by-sell-by-and-best-by-dates

Zarate, M. (2021, March 24). *The Young Adult's Guide to Cooking 101.* lifestylefrisco.com. https://lifestylefrisco.com/the-young-adults-guide-to-cooking-101/

Meredith, D. (2023, January 30). *42 Easy Breakfast Ideas with 5 Ingredients or Less.* Taste of Home. https://www.tasteofhome.com/collection/5-ingredient-easy-breakfast-ideas/

Loewentheil, H. (2021, December 15). *29 Easy Lunch Recipes That Take Ten Minutes Or Less.* BuzzFeed. https://www.buzzfeed.com/hannahloewentheil/10-minute-lunch-recipes

Sara @ Gathering Dreams. (2022, October 25). *50+ Quick And Easy Dinner Recipes (30 minutes or Less)*. Gathering Dreams. https://gathering-dreams.com/quick-easy-dinner-recipes/

Chapter Two

Older adolescent (15 to 19 years) and young adult (20 to 24 years) mortality. (2022, January 28). https://www.who.int/news-room/fact-sheets/detail/levels-and-trends-in-older-adolescent-(15-to-19-years)-and-young-adult-(20-to-24-years)-mortality

How to handle 10 common home emergencies. (n.d.). The Grange Insurance. https://www.grangeinsurance.com/tips/how-to-handle-home-emergencies

What to do if you choke while you're alone. (n.d.). https://www.parkview.com/community/dashboard/what-to-do-if-you-choke-while-youre-alone

Choking: First aid. (2022, October 11). Mayo Clinic. https://www.mayoclinic.org/first-aid/first-aid-choking/basics/art-20056637

Top 10 Road Emergencies and How to Handle Them | FleetCardsUSA. (n.d.). FleetCardUSA. https://fleetcardsusa.com/blog/top-10-road-emergencies-and-how-to-handle-them/

Street Smart Teens—National Crime Prevention Council. (n.d.). http://archive.ncpc.org/programs/teens-crime-and-the-community/monthly-article/street-smart-teens.html

Chapter Three

Keech, D. (2022, October 31). *15 Home Maintenance Tasks and Repairs Everyone Should Know How to Do.* https://blog.militarybyowner.com/15-home-maintenance-tasks-and-repairs-everyone-should-know-how-to-do

Ravenscraft, E., & Newton, A. A. (2021, May 14). *The Most Common Home Repairs You Can Easily Handle Yourself.* Lifehacker. https://lifehacker.com/the-most-common-home-repairs-you-can-easily-do-yourself-1445435125

Paudyal, N. (2016, March 13). *10 Basic Car Repairs Everyone Should Know.* Lifehack. https://www.lifehack.org/374885/10-basic-car-repairs-everyone-should-know

Sulpy, E. (2022, December 8). *How to Teach Basic Car Maintenance to Your Teen | GetJerry.com.* https://getjerry.com/advice/how-to-teach-basic-car-maintenance-to-your-teen-by-elaine-sulpy

Anderberg, J. (2021, August 22). *Keep Your House in Tip-Top Shape: An Incredibly Handy Home Maintenance Checklist.* The Art of Manliness. https://www.artofmanliness.com/lifestyle/homeownership/keep-your-house-in-tip-top-shape-an-incredibly-handy-home-maintenance-checklist/

Chapter Four

Brenner, B., PhD. (2021, April 24). *The Importance of Mental Wellbeing in Young Adults.* Therapy Group of NYC. https://nyctherapy.com/therapists-nyc-blog/the-importance-of-mental-wellbeing-in-young-adults/

Berthold, J. (2022, April 13). *48% of Young Adults Struggled with Mental Health in Mid-2021.* UCSF. https://www.ucsf.edu/news/2022/04/422611/48-young-adults-struggled-mental-health-mid-2021

GoodTherapy, B. (2022, January 31). *What's the Connection Between Physical Health and Mental Health?* GoodTherapy.org Therapy Blog. https://www.goodtherapy.org/blog/whats-the-connection-between-physical-health-and-mental-health/

10 mental health awareness tips for older teens and young adults. (2022, June 30). https://www.michiganmedicine.org/health-lab/10-mental-health-awareness-tips-older-teens-and-young-adults

Owens, E. (2023, January 25). *You Are Enough - 10 Things That Don't Define Your Worth.* Antimaximalist. https://antimaximalist.com/you-are-enough/

Dube, P. (2022, May 12). *19 Best Foods for Physical and Mental Wellbeing.* Blog - HealthifyMe. https://www.healthifyme.com/blog/19-best-foods-for-physical-and-mental-wellbeing/

The Best Types of Exercise for Mental Health. (2022, August 1). GeneSight. https://genesight.com/blog/patient/the-best-types-of-exercise-for-mental-health/

Canadian Mental Health Association. (2020). *How can I take care of my physical health?* Here to Help. https://www.heretohelp.bc.ca/q-and-a/how-can-i-take-care-of-my-physical-health

Unknown, F. (2021, May 6). *How to take care of your mental health | 10 effective tips.* FutureLearn. https://www.futurelearn.com/info/blog/how-to-take-care-of-your-mental-health

Scott, S. (2022, November 3). *17 Mindfulness Activities and Exercises for Teens in 2023.* Happier Human. https://www.happierhuman.com/mindfulness-activities-teenagers/

Chapter Five

Page 404, Latest News, Latest Headlines. (2020, December 18). https://www.indiatoday.in/education-today/featurephilia/story/4-reasons-financial-education-is-important-at-a-young-age-1750907-2020-12-18+https:/www.spaceship.com.au/learn/smarter-saving-tips-for-young-adults

Basic Budgeting Tips Everyone Should Know. (2022, September 15). The Balance. https://www.thebalancemoney.com/budgeting-101-1289589

Khalfani-Cox, L. (n.d.). *10 Steps to Be Debt-Free in Less Than a Year.* AARP. https://www.aarp.org/money/credit-loans-debt/info-07-2013/10-steps-to-becoming-debtfree-in-less-than-a-year.html

Brown, D. (2022, September 19). *Reasons To Invest at an Early Age | CAG.* Coastal Advice Group. https://coastaladvicegroup.com.au/invest-at-an-early-age/

The Advantages of Investing When You're Young. (2022, June 26). The Balance. https://www.thebalancemoney.com/the-advantages-of-investing-in-your-20s-5179604

Baker, B. (2022, November 14). *A guide to mutual fund investing.* Bankrate. https://www.bankrate.com/investing/guide-to-mutual-funds/

Esajian, P. (2022, August 17). *Real Estate Investing For Beginners: Everything You Need To Know.* FortuneBuilders. https://www.fortunebuilders.com/investing-in-real-estate-for-beginners/

Plummer, S. (2022, October 5). *How to Make Money with Life Insurance (2023).* The Annuity Expert. https://www.annuityexpertadvice.com/how-to-make-money-with-life-insurance/

Frankel, M. C. (2022, December 22). *How to Invest in Stocks: A Beginner's Guide for Getting Started.* The Motley Fool. https://www.fool.com/investing/how-to-invest/stocks/

How To Invest Money In ULIP? (2022, November 11). Kotak Life. https://www.kotaklife.com/insurance-guide/wealth-creation/how-to-invest-money-in-ulip

Shaikh, A. (2022, October 21). *Wise Investment Ideas for Young Adults*. Youth Incorporated Magazine. https://youthincmag.com/wise-investment-ideas-for-young-adults

Chapter Six

Pandit, P. (2020, May 2). *Importance Of Interpersonal Skills*. Learn From Blogs. https://learnfromblogs.com/importance-of-interpersonal-skills

(c) Copyright skillsyouneed.com 2011-2023. (n.d.). *Interpersonal Skills | SkillsYouNeed*. https://www.skillsyouneed.com/interpersonal-skills.html

Birt, J. (2022, August 10). *10 Effective Ways To Improve Verbal Communication Skills*. Indeed. https://www.indeed.com/career-advice/career-development/how-to-improve-verbal-communication-skills

6 Ways to Improve Your Non-verbal Communication Skills. (2018, June 18). Mental Health First Aid. https://www.mentalhealthfirstaid.org/external/2018/06/6-ways-to-improve-your-non-verbal-communication-skills/

Barnard, D. (2021, March 3). *How to Develop Effective Verbal Communication Skills*. https://virtualspeech.com/blog/verbal-communication-skills

Improving Emotional Intelligence (EQ). (n.d.). HelpGuide.org. https://www.helpguide.org/articles/mental-health/emotional-intelligence-eq.htm

BetterHelp Editorial Team. (2023, January 5). *7 Tips To Help You Improve Your Teamwork Skills | BetterHelp*. https://www.betterhelp.com/advice/teamwork/7-tips-to-help-you-improve-your-teamwork-skills/

Learning Resources: Employability Skills: Employability. (n.d.). https://libguides.wigan-leigh.ac.uk/c.php?g=667800

Shields, A. (2020, October 15). *3 Mediation Skills To Help Navigate Conflict In Times Of Uncertainty*. Forbes. https://www.forbes.com/sites/annashields/2020/10/15/3-mediation-skills-to-help-navigate-conflict-in-times-of-uncertainty/?sh=10e80d37f18e

How to Improve Your Problem-Solving Skills? (2022, May 10). Top Universities. https://www.topuniversities.com/blog/how-improve-your-problem-solving-skills

Dsouza, M. (2020, December 11). *How to Make Better Decisions with 7 Fearless Steps*. Productive Club. https://productiveclub.com/improve-decision-making-skills/

therapistaid.com. (2016). *Assertive Communication*. https://www.therapistaid.com/worksheets/assertive-communication

Chapter Seven

Jigsaw Young People's Health In Mind. (2022, December 5). *Goal setting*. Jigsaw. https://jigsaw.ie/goal-setting/

Lynch, M. (2022, October 25). *What Is Goal Setting And How It Leads to a Fulfilling Life*. Lifehack. https://www.lifehack.org/articles/lifestyle/goal-setting-the-why-behind-the-what.html

Start Finding Your Purpose and Unlock Your Best Life. (n.d.). https://www.betterup.com/blog/finding-purpose

How to Set Goals and Achieve Them: 10 Strategies for Success. (n.d.). https://www.betterup.com/blog/how-to-set-goals-and-achieve-them

Morrison, L. L. (2016, March 16). *Effective Time Management Strategies for Young Adults*. Lizmorrisontherapy. https://www.lizmorrisontherapy.com/post/2016/03/16/effective-time-management-strategies-for-young-adults

Adegbuyi, F. (2022, January 10). *How to Organize Your Life*. Ambition & Balance. https://blog.doist.com/organize-your-life/

Chapter Eight

The Difference Between a Career and a Job and Why it's Important. (n.d.). CWA. https://cwa.ac.uk/about/alumni/alumni-news/the-difference-between-a-career-and-a-job-and-why-its-important

Pant, S. (2020, June 16). *Why is career planning important at an early stage?* India Today. https://www.indiatoday.in/education-today/featurephilia/story/why-is-career-planning-important-at-an-early-stage-1689512-2020-06-16

Herrity, J. (2022, July 1). *How To Choose the Career Path That's Right for You*. Indeed. https://www.indeed.com/career-advice/finding-a-job/how-to-choose-a-career

Successful Career Planning | Fredonia.edu. (n.d.). https://www.fredonia.edu/student-life/career-development-office/successful-career-planning

Dowdy, L. C. (2015, September 8). *Young Money: Four Secrets of Career Success in Early Work Years*. NBC News. https://www.nbcnews.com/better/careers/young-money-four-secrets-career-success-early-work-years-n423371

Indeed Editorial Team. (2020, December 8). *5 Steps to Create a Career Development Plan for Yourself*. Indeed. https://www.indeed.com/career-advice/career-development/steps-to-create-a-career-development-plan

www.ingramcontent.com/pod-product-compliance
Lightning Source LLC
Chambersburg PA
CBHW071345080526
44587CB00017B/2975